# Contents

I0480212

THE RHYTHM WAVE: Six Laws to Build a Leadership System Without Heroes

Kevin Cover

2025

*Copyright © 2025 Kevin Cover*

Copyright © 2025 Kevin Cover All rights reserved.

ISBN (ebook): 978-1-967765-08-9
For the people who trusted me long before I understood why that mattered. For my family, who gave me strength. And for every leader who has ever carried more than they know.

# Author's Note

I did not grow up reading leadership books. I did not study management theory. I was not the kid highlighting insights from business gurus. I read Nelson DeMille, John Grisham, and the occasional FBI or murder mystery. Straightforward stories. Consequences. Cause and effect.

That matters because this book came the same way.

I did not come to leadership through books or classrooms. I came to it through pressure.

Car dealerships. Call centers. Membership businesses. Higher education. Teams that needed to perform—whether I was ready or not.

This is not a sales book. These are sales stories, because that is where I learned what holds and what breaks. The principles underneath them are about leading people. Any people. In any environment.

Over thirty-five years, I watched the same pattern repeat itself.

When things were working, leaders became the system. When things broke, everyone waited for them to fix it.

At first, I thought that was what leadership was supposed to look like. Be available. Be decisive. Be the one who carries it when it gets heavy.

What I learned instead is that carrying everything does not make you strong. It makes the system fragile.

This book came from years of trying to build teams that did not depend on me being in every room, every deal, every decision. Teams that could hold steady without adrenaline or rescues.

I did not invent what follows. I noticed it. Across industries and roles, the same conditions showed up whenever performance stabilized. The same conditions were missing whenever it collapsed.

Those patterns became principles. The principles became a system.

That system is what you are holding.

# Orientation

In every system, there is a point where movement slows.

Sometimes it is a process. Sometimes it is a rule. Often, it is a person.

When progress depends on a single point, the system becomes fragile. Decisions wait. Energy hesitates. Confidence concentrates instead of spreading.

This is not a character flaw. It is a design problem.

Most systems drift here without intention. Success masks the dependency. Results delay the warning. By the time strain is felt, the pattern is already set.

This book is about identifying where dependency lives and redesigning the system, so movement does not rely on presence.

Not faster. Not louder. Not through effort or force.

But through rhythm.

The wave does not reward urgency. It rewards return.

# The Rhythm Leader vs. The Hero Leader

Every leader faces a choice. Will you be the Hero, or will you build the Rhythm? Figure 1: Hero Leader vs. Rhythm Leader

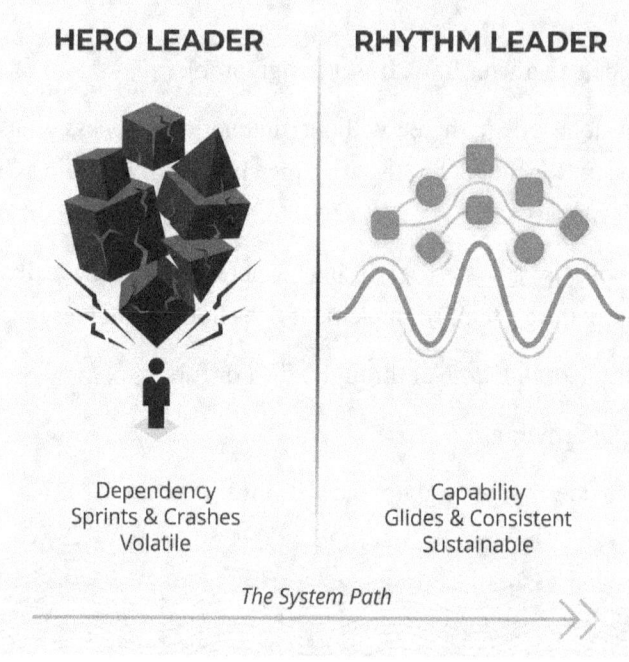

*Figure 1: Hero Leader vs. Rhythm Leader*

## The Hero Leader

The Hero fixes. The Hero rescues. The Hero burns. You provide the adrenaline; they provide the dependency. It's a cage dressed up as respect.

They are the first ones in and the last ones out. They take the hardest calls. They close the biggest deals. They handle the most difficult students. They run every important meeting. They make every critical decision. They step in when others fail.

And their team learns to wait for the rescue.

When the hero wins, they take the credit. When they lose, they demand more grind. Their performance is volatile. Their team is exhausted. Their organization cannot scale past their own voice. The Hero cannot take a vacation without everything falling apart. Cannot delegate without worrying that it will not get done right.

Heroes do not create capability. They create dependency.

And dependency is not loyalty. It is learned helplessness dressed up as respect.

This shows up everywhere: The salesperson who will not let anyone else touch their accounts.

The teacher who believes no one else can handle their classroom.

The coach who calls every play because he does not trust their team to think.

The parent who micromanages every homework assignment because they are terrified their kid will fail.

The executive who bottlenecks every decision because he or she believes no one else will get it right.

The pattern is universal. The cost is universal.

Hero culture is the single most celebrated cause of organizational failure. Every level rewards it. Every leadership myth reinforces it. And the people it destroys protect it longest.

## The Rhythm Leader

The Rhythm Leader understands that systems outlast heroes.

They do not chase emergencies; they build cadence.

They coach their team through The Box instead of solving everything themselves. They celebrate the weekly flow, not the one-time rescue.

They teach people to diagnose problems, not report them.

To recognize patterns, not react to symptoms.

To maintain rhythm, not hit numbers.

Their performance is consistent.

Their team is confident.

Their organization grows without them.

The Rhythm Leader can take two weeks off and return to a system that has grown stronger in their absence.

They can promote people without losing bench strength. Can scale to fifty people using the same frameworks that worked with five.

In a rhythm-based system, the process is the star.

Not the hero. Not the founder. Not the charismatic teacher.

Not the star closer. Not the one person everyone relies on.

The process.

This works whether you are building a sales organization, running a school, coaching a team, leading a division, or raising a family.

The principles do not change.

Build the rhythm. Protect the rhythm. Scale the rhythm.

## The Choice

If you are tired of being the one who always has to close, teach, fix, decide, or rescue...

If you are burned out from being the emotional engine of your organization... If you want something that scales beyond your personal brilliance... Keep reading.

Here is what I learned over three decades without mentors, without training, and without shortcuts:

# The Six Laws

Every organization I have been part of followed the same arc.

Different industries. Different people. Same outcomes.

When things were strong, they felt smooth. When they broke, they felt sudden. They were neither.

Performance follows conditions. When the conditions are right, progress continues without force. When they are wrong, effort increases and results fade.

The Six Laws are not steps or best practices. They are patterns that were present whenever a system held together and absent whenever it did not.

I did not discover them by studying success. I recognized them by studying collapse.

Law 6: Collapse Success hides fragility until the system breaks.

Law 5: Reciprocity Ownership must move or momentum stalls.

Law 4: Momentum Invisible progress kills confidence.

Law 3: Rhythm Cadence outlasts intensity.

Law 2: The Box—Stalled decisions are missing something specific.

Law 1: ICE—Influence moves in order. Like. Trust. Understand.

## Why the Laws Are a Wave, Not a Ladder

The Six Laws in this book are not steps. They form an interdependent system.

A wave.

Law 1 builds influence.

Law 2 handles resistance.

Law 3 creates consistency. Laws 4 through 6 protect what you build.

Rhythm compounds. Urgency exhausts. Maintenance beats rescue.

You do not climb them once. You ride them, maintain them, and adjust them.

Systems require maintenance. They require you to return to Law 1 even while installing Law 5, because trust is not built in a single step. Rhythm does not hold itself.

The wave never stops.

When you learn to ride it, it carries you forward.

## The Rhythm Wave System Map

THE FOUNDATION: Influence, Confidence, Empathy

This is where trust begins.

THE ENGINE: The Box, Rhythm This is where consistency lives.

THE PROTECTIVE OUTCOMES: Momentum, Reciprocity, Collapse This is where systems survive their founders.

This is the operating system you will build.

Not a tactic. Not a trick.

A system that works whether or not you are in the room.

## Quick Diagnostic

Three questions. Answer them honestly.

Does performance drop when you step away? That is Collapse.

Does effort reset daily instead of compounding? That is Momentum missing.

Does ownership flow in one direction? That is Reciprocity broken.

If you answered yes to any of these, the system is not finished. This book shows you how to finish it.

## What You Will Learn

By the end of this book, you will know how to:

Build trust without manipulation (The Sequence / ICE) Diagnose and solve objections using a single tool Reverse-engineer outcomes Create consistency through weekly cadence Earn permission before you ask Protect your system from drift The goal is not to be impressive.

The goal is to be unnecessary.

When your system works without you, you have won.

## How to Read This Book

The stories that follow are not included to persuade you. They are included because this is where these laws revealed themselves.

If you recognize your own environment in what comes next, that will not be a coincidence. It will be pattern recognition.

This book is not written for leaders trying to move faster. It is written for leaders who want things to hold.

If that matters to you, keep reading.

## Where This System Has Been Tested

I have spent thirty-five years building teams across five industries. Not studying them. Building them. What follows is a summary of where this system has operated and what it produced.

Automotive retail. I started selling cars at Huntington Honda in 1991 with no training, no mentor, and no playbook. Within two years I was the top salesperson in the dealership. Salesperson of the Year three consecutive years. Not from pressure. From learning to read people before they spoke. I moved to Greenwich Acura as General Manager, where I ran all operations including sales, service, and team development.

Franchise operations. I owned and operated three DirectBuy franchise locations in New York and Boston. Three of the top ten performing franchises nationally. The number one location in the country for several consecutive years. The sales process I built was adopted by 160 franchises nationwide. The system scaled because it did not depend on me being in the room. Travel and membership sales. At International Cruise and Excursions, I partnered with the division president to build a face-to-face sales division from concept to over twenty million dollars in annual revenue. We expanded from one location to six sales offices and twenty-eight marketing partners across multiple states. Consistent twenty percent year-over-year growth from inception through the final phase. That growth did not come from heroics. It came from installing rhythm at distance.

Higher education. As Vice President of Campus Admissions at a publicly traded higher education company, I directed over one hundred team members across fifteen campuses and ten areas of study. The team delivered ten percent average annual growth in new student enrollment and revenue for three consecutive years. Channel revenue increased fifteen percent in a single fiscal year. When the company reduced compensation by fifteen percent, we maintained team engagement and productivity by leading through the transition instead of managing around it. The system held because the system was the point—not the person running it.

Five industries. Thirty-five years. Teams ranging from four people to over one hundred. The conditions changed every time. The principles did not.

This book is the result.

# PART I: THE ORIGIN STORIES

# Introduction: The Shoelace Test

"I can tell if you are going to close a sale by watching you tie your shoes."

Not because I am psychic. Not because I had insider training. But because of something that emerged in a Honda showroom in the 1990s, on my own, with no one teaching me what to look for.

Trust is not built in the close. It is built in the shoelace.

This book is about invisible moments.

The small cues that reveal whether someone trusts you before they ever say yes or no. The difference between being liked and being trusted. The signals that separate top performers from nice people who finish last.

The shoelace test taught me something no sales manager ever taught me. Trust shows up in how people move. Who follows? Who waits? Who synchronizes? Who does not?

When a prospect trusts you, they mirror your pace. They let you lead. They relax into your rhythm. When they do not, they stay guarded. They keep a distance.

Once you learn to read these signals, everything changes. And here is what matters: this is not about sales.

This pattern plays out everywhere. Classrooms, boardrooms, coaching fields, living rooms. Students mirror teachers they trust. Teams bring problems early to executives they trust. Players synchronize with coaches they trust. Kids open up with parents they trust. The environments change. The signals do not. On Zoom, trust shows up in posture and pace. On the phone, in breath matching and timing. In email, in tone, clarity, and speed.

No tricks. No scripts. No manufactured urgency.

Rhythm, trust, and authentic influence.

Every origin story in this section reveals the early patterns of rhythm, trust, and influence forming long before I had names for them.

# Chapter 1: Mistakes & Discovery (Honda, 1991–1995)

## HONDA ERA: BECOMING AWARE

I walked into Huntington Honda expecting to learn how to sell. What I didn't expect was how quickly I would learn what I didn't want to become.

The culture wasn't built on integrity or care. Pressure and manipulation built it. Every day, who could push the hardest, hold the line longest? Profit was the only point.

I stood there some mornings, watching it all unfold, wondering if I was the only one who got sick of it. I didn't want to be "that guy." But I was afraid of something even worse: failing.

That fear sat with me. Fear of being fired, not paying rent, and not being good enough. Stuck between my values and my paycheck. That internal collision between pressure and integrity would shape everything that came after.

I felt lost.

Because I wanted to succeed. I wanted to win. I wanted to prove something to myself. But I couldn't succeed the way everyone around me was willing to.

And no one was offering an alternative.

Mentors didn't exist. Neither did guides. No examples of "doing it the right way and still making it." Only noise, pressure, tension, and tactics I couldn't bring myself to use.

So, I learned by watching, not the techniques, but the people. Not the scripts, but the behavior. Not the pitches, but the moments before the pitch—where truth leaked out.

I noticed small things other people ignored: When someone's eyes softened.

When their shoulders tightened.

When their voice sped up to hide discomfort. When they were friendly but didn't trust us.

When they hesitated because something felt wrong.

I didn't have a framework for any of this yet. I didn't even have a plan.

What I had was a simple question that grew louder every day: "How do I succeed without becoming someone I can't respect?" That question forced me to pay attention to the real patterns underneath the chaos.

People make emotional decisions first.

People protect themselves when they don't feel safe.

People tell the truth when you're quiet long enough to hear it. People trust the person who makes them feel understood, not pressured.

People lean into rhythm and recoil from force.

I didn't have names for any of it yet. But the patterns were stacking.

A way to sell without manipulation.

A way to help people move forward without pushing them.

A way to earn enough to survive and eventually thrive. Without losing my integrity.

Honda was where I decided that success built on pressure wasn't the success I wanted. If I wanted a career I could be proud of, I'd have to build a system no one had shown me.

Honda didn't teach me the answer. Honda taught me the cost of not having one.

---

**LESSON IN A BREATH**

*Integrity without capability leads to fear. Capability without integrity leads to regret. Sales cultures built on pressure create compliance, not trust. Systems built out of necessity outlast systems built under pressure.*

---

Integrity without capability leads to fear. Capability without integrity leads to regret. Sales cultures built on pressure create compliance, not trust. Systems built out of necessity outlast systems built under pressure.

**Endnotes:**

[1] Nonverbal Trust & Emotional Cues In my experience, people display emotional and trust signals before verbalizing them through hesitation, micro-expressions, and body tension. [2] Behavior Reveals Discomfort Before Words Do Emotional states show through pacing, tone, and micro-movements before the conscious mind forms the language to express them. [3] Manipulation Erodes Trust Faster Than Poor Communication. When people feel tricked, they become less open and trusting, which stops progress.

# PHASE 1: MISTAKES & DISCOVERY

How the patterns were discovered, without mentors, without shortcuts, and without anyone showing me where to look.

# The Friend Zone

Falling off a cloud is nothing compared to hitting concrete. Winning feels light. Losing? You feel it in your chest. Empty showroom. Quiet phone. Team stops paying attention.

Three weeks into a dry spell. Tuesday afternoon, nothing was happening. Heat shimmering off Jericho Turnpike. Me and the hum of the overhead lights. When nobody's buying from you, and everyone else is closing, when you can hear them laughing in the break room about their morning sales, you notice things. The shine on the linoleum. Old coffee sitting in the pot, burned and dark. How the other guy's sound when they're walking someone to finance, that confident rhythm in their voice.

Success moves. It has momentum. Failure sits still. And when it's sitting still, when you're stuck watching everyone else succeed, you either figure out what's off or you stay stuck forever.

The ones who make it through, who get better from it, they're the ones who stay level. Good day, bad day, doesn't matter. They don't ride too high when it's going well. Don't fall apart when it's not. They keep something steady. That steadiness—calm over chaos—was my first unconscious brush with rhythm.

Something about staying calm when you wanted to panic. About not getting too excited or too crushed. About figuring out what was happening inside you before you could control what was happening in front of you.

I filed that away. It would matter more than I knew.

And for a while, before I figured any of that out, I thought being liked was the total game.

## The Golden Retriever Lesson

When I began selling cars, I was twenty-two and convinced that charm equaled success. If people liked me, they'd buy from me. So, I made it my mission to be the nicest guy on the lot. I smiled through the rain, fetched coffees without being asked, laughed too hard at their jokes. I was a golden retriever with a clipboard, eager and desperate for approval.

And it worked, sort of. People loved me. They told me so. But they didn't buy from me. One couple looking at an Accord. Forty-five minutes with them. Got them water bottles from the vending machine. The husband clapped me on the shoulder and said, "You've been helpful, kid." I expected the close. Then they asked for a minute to talk privately. When they came back, the woman smiled and said, "We're going to think about it and come back tomorrow." Three days later, I saw that same Accord rolling off the lot with another salesperson's name on the paperwork. When I asked him what happened, he shrugged. "They called me directly. Said they wanted someone who was more experienced." I'd given them everything. He got the sale. I got a handshake.

That's when I stopped chasing approval and started figuring out what made people believe you.

## The Prelude Incident

Young couple, silver Prelude. They laughed at my jokes, nodded through the pitch. We vibed. Test drove the car. When we got back, she looked at him and said, "Babe, I love it." We sat down. I ran the numbers. He looked at her and said, "Let's do it." Then they stood up. "We left our checkbook at home. We're gonna run back and grab it. Be back in thirty minutes." I shook their hands. Waved as they pulled out of the lot. Thirty minutes passed. Then an hour. Then two. They never came back.

**LESSON IN A BREATH**

*Being liked fills your ego. Being trusted fills your calendar. The friend zone in sales happens when people feel safe with you but not confident in you. This story plants the seed of Law 1: ICE, the gap between being liked and being trusted.*

Being liked fills your ego. Being trusted fills your calendar. The friend zone in sales happens when people feel safe with you but not confident in you. This story plants the seed of Law 1: ICE, the gap between being liked and being trusted.

## The Shoelace Test

The first real breakthrough happened by accident. I walked a couple out to an Accord on a Thursday afternoon, and my shoelace came undone. We talked, laughing about something I don't even remember, and I stopped mid-stride to tie it. Dropped on one knee right there on the asphalt. They stopped too. Stood there waiting for me, not saying anything, not checking their watches. Waited.

I thought little of it until a couple of days later, when the same thing happened with a different couple, except they kept walking. Didn't even look back. Didn't slow down. Kept going toward their car like I wasn't there, like I'd never existed. Like I was part of the scenery.

That difference stuck with me. I kept replaying both moments. Why did one couple stop, and the other didn't? Same lot, same kind of prospects, roughly the same point in the walk. What was different?

I tested it. Not shoelaces every time. I'd adjust a price tag. Check my clipboard. Straighten a door mirror. Crouched down like I saw a scratch or something on the paint. Small stops, nothing dramatic, never more than a few seconds. And I'd watch what they did.

Some people immediately stopped with me, as if it were automatic. Others kept moving as if I were invisible, as if they'd already forgotten I was there.

Here's what happened: the ones who stopped almost always bought. The ones who didn't rarely bought. This tiny behavioral split was my first actual glimpse of influence before information. It wasn't about the car. Wasn't about the price or how good my pitch was or whether they liked the color. It was about whether they were following me or tolerating me.

Trust isn't something people announce. It's something you see in how they move, how they respond when you change direction or pause.

I used it with every prospect. If they stopped, I had something real. If they didn't, I hadn't earned it yet.

Guy with a Civic. Mid-forties, clean-cut. Asked good questions. We did the test drive, and he was fine, nodding along. We came back, and I started walking him toward my desk to run numbers. About halfway across the lot, I stopped to check a tire. Bent down, ran my hand along the tread.

He kept walking. Didn't even break stride. Didn't look back.

I caught up with him, and we sat down anyway. Spent 20 minutes running numbers and showing him options. He smiled, nodded, and said he'd think about it. Never came back. Never called. Wasted time. I knew it the second he walked past me at the tire. But I still didn't trust what I was seeing. After that, I trusted it.

## Matching Pace

Then I saw the pace. The speed at which people walked. It sounds like nothing, like the smallest detail possible, but it mattered more than I ever would've guessed.

I'm naturally a fast walker. When I was in my golden retriever phase, I'd walk prospects out to the lot like I was late for something. Quick steps, clipboard tucked under my arm, pointing at cars while speed-walking past them.

Older couple, Accord on the back row. Hot afternoon, eighty-five degrees. I moved at my normal pace. About halfway there, the husband breathed hard, laboring, trying to keep up with me. His wife was a few steps behind him, falling further back. Both shoulders tight, faces flushed, not talking, trying not to lose me.

When we got to the car, they were both winded.

I didn't close that deal. They left twenty minutes later, polite but distant.

After that, I began paying attention to how people moved. Some walked fast, crisp and purposeful. Some strolled, taking their time. Some wandered with no particular rhythm at all. And I began matching their pace instead of leading at my own.

When I slowed my pace to match theirs, everything changed. Conversations got easier. The tension dropped. People relaxed. They asked more questions, better questions. And they bought more often.

It was the same thing as the shoelace test. Synchronization. When two people are in rhythm, everything flows. When you're out of sync, there's friction, even if nobody says anything out loud.

I tested it for weeks. Let them set the tempo. The buyers who matched my stride, or who I matched, closed at about 70%. The ones where we were out of sync? Maybe twenty percent.

One couple, mid-thirties, came in on a Saturday afternoon. High energy. Talked fast, moved fast, laughing and joking with each other. I walked fast. I talked fast. I matched their pace, and we moved through the lot like we were late for something. It felt chaotic, almost frantic, but it worked. They fed off the energy. We did a test drive where the guy was grinning the whole time, and when we got back, he said, "Let's do it." That same day, they drove off in a new Accord.

Next prospect: complete opposite. Older guy, late sixties, alone. Moved like he had all day. I slowed way down. Matched his pace exactly. We spent forty-five minutes walking the lot together. Talked very little. He'd stop, look at a car for a while, and move on. I stayed with him, quiet, no pressure. Eventually, he stopped at a Passport and said, "Tell me about this one." That moment—slowing down enough to match his world instead of pulling him into mine—was one of the earliest emotional fingerprints of rhythm, long before I could name it.

We talked for ten minutes. He bought it.

Same day. Two totally different rhythms. Both closed because I matched the tempo instead of forcing mine.

Teachers see the same thing in classrooms. Coaches see it on fields. Parents with kids. You can lose people before you ever get to the message if you're moving at the wrong speed. Pacing is equally important on Teams or Zoom meetings and on phone calls.

---

**LESSON IN A BREATH**

*Trust shows in movement; people reveal commitment through rhythm, not words. People who stop when you stop are following; those who don't are tolerating*

---

Trust shows in movement; people reveal commitment through rhythm, not words. People who stop when you stop are following; those who don't are tolerating

### Endnotes: The Shoelace Test

[1] Behavioral Synchrony and Trust Chartrand, T. L. & Bargh, J. A. "The Chameleon Effect," Journal of Personality and Social Psychology. Physical coordination between individuals predicts

relationship quality and trust more accurately than self-reported measures. [2] Nonverbal Compliance as Buying Signal In sales environments, nonverbal compliance is an early indicator of leadership acceptance and buying intent. [3] Postural Mirroring and Rapport LaFrance, M. "Postural Mirroring and Rapport," Interaction Rhythms. Interpersonal synchronization in walking pace, speaking tempo, and gestural mimicry accompanies rapport, persuasion success, and relationship satisfaction. - Adaptive Pacing and Close Rates Adaptive pacing strategies in sales interactions improve close rates across diverse prospect demographics and personality types.

## The Power of Silence

Figure 2: The Power of Silence

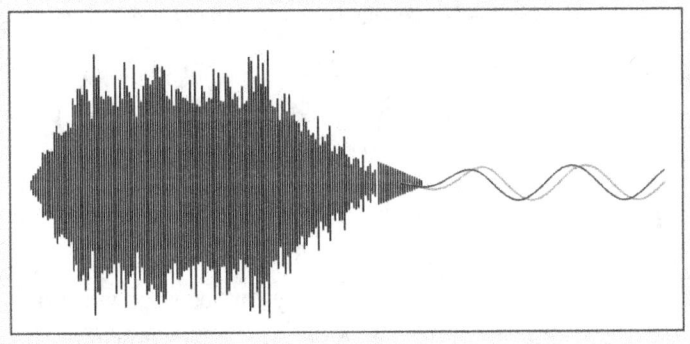

**THE POWER OF SILENCE**

BPM: 60 | STABLE

*"Silence creates the space where truth emerges."*

*Figure 2: The Power of Silence*

My favorite discovery came from being exhausted. I'd done five test drives back-to-back. It was late afternoon, July heat still thick, and I had nothing left. My voice was shot. My energy was gone. I ran on fumes.

A husband and wife came in to look at a used minivan. They had three kids in tow and a dog that wouldn't stop barking in the crate in the back. They were tired, distracted, and clearly overwhelmed.

I launched into my pitch like a machine gun: features, warranty, why this was the perfect family vehicle, how the payment would fit their budget, and how we could take their trade today. I talked for twelve straight minutes without breathing.

When I finally stopped, there was total silence.

Not the good kind.

The husband looked at his wife. The wife looked at the floor. One kid started crying. Then the husband said, "We're going to think about it," and they walked out.

I stood there stunned. I had crushed the presentation. I knew I had. Every feature, every benefit, every logical reason to buy. I nailed it.

I reflected on what I missed and said to myself. "Kevin, try shutting up next time." This was the first time I saw how influence collapses when information overwhelms it—a pattern.

The following weekend, the same thing happened, another family, same used car, same chaotic energy. But this time, after the greeting and a few rapport questions ("How many car seats are we fitting back there?"), I shut my mouth. I let them talk. I let them tell me about soccer practice, the dog that chewed the old minivan seats, and the teenager who got his permit. I nodded. I smiled. I asked one follow-up question and then... nothing.

Silence.

Ten seconds.

The silence stretched.

Finally, the wife looked at her husband and said, "This is the one, isn't it?" Twenty minutes later, they were in finance signing papers. No discounts. No pushing. No logical onslaught.

Silence after connection.

The most powerful close in sales isn't a technique. It's the moment you stop talking and let the trust you've built do the work.

From that Saturday forward, silence became my sharpest tool. Not awkward silence but earned silence. The kind that only exists after someone feels genuinely heard.

The best leaders and closers I've ever known aren't the ones with the best scripts.

They're the ones who discovered that sometimes the most powerful thing you can say... is nothing at all.

---

**LESSON IN A BREATH**

*The close begins when you stop talking. Silence after a genuine connection is the most powerful close in existence*

---

The close begins when you stop talking. Silence after a genuine connection is the most powerful close in existence

## The Friday Close

Friday night, a couple came in thirty minutes before close. Everyone else was cleaning up, counting their commissions, ready to go home. It had been a long week for all of us. A few guys saw the couple pull into the lot and literally walked to the back to avoid them. Disappeared. I watched them do it.

I was halfway out the door myself, keys in hand. Tired. My feet hurt. But something told me to stay.

I walked out. Forties, exhausted. She carried a Target bag. He wore dusty work boots and stained pants. They looked like they'd been working all day, and this was their only window.

They said they were looking and might come back tomorrow. That line. I'd heard it a hundred times.

I slowed my pace. Asked questions instead of pitching. They'd been car shopping for two weeks, at four dealerships. Nobody gave them the time of day. They kept getting brushed off because they "didn't look like buyers." That's what one salesperson told them. Too tired. Too blue-collar. Wrong zip code, probably. But they were pre-approved for financing. Had their paperwork ready. They kept getting dismissed before anyone bothered to find that out. Underneath all the bias and dismissal was a simple problem. Nobody had slowed down long enough to find out what they were actually afraid of.

I stopped to tie my shoe. Dropped on one knee right there on the lot. They stopped with me. Didn't keep walking. They didn't check their watches. Waited.

I already knew.

We walked through the lot together. Slow. No rush. No pressure. I matched their deliberate, careful pace. They weren't in a hurry. They tried to make a good decision after a long day. I listened more than I talked. Asked what they needed. What mattered to them? What they were worried about.

After about fifteen minutes, I stopped next to a Civic and adjusted the price sheet on the windshield, as if I were checking something. They stopped too. Stood there with me. That was it. They were with me. Not tolerating me.

We went inside. Sat down in my cubicle. The showroom was almost empty now, with the overhead lights humming, and one other salesperson finishing paperwork at his desk. I asked them, "What's most important to you right now?" Silence.

The husband looked at his wife. She looked down at her hands. Then he looked back at me and said, "Honestly? We've had a rough year. Lost some income. We're scared of overspending. We need a car, but we can't afford to make a mistake." That was it. The truth. The thing they'd probably been carrying into every dealership—the fear nobody else had bothered to ask about. At that moment, one honest question surfaces the real hesitation, rather than wrestling with excuses. I walked them through the numbers. Calm. No hype. No pressure. No fast-talking or trying to upsell them into something bigger. I showed them exactly what it would cost per month. Explained the warranty in plain language. Answered every question they had, and they had a lot. Gave them space to think, to talk to each other quietly while I stepped away for a minute.

They bought the car. Came back the next day with a cashier's check and drove off.

Before they left that night, the husband shook my hand and said something I'll never forget. He said, "You're easy to buy from." Not easy to talk to. Not friendly. Easy to buy from.

That line changed everything I was figuring out.

Control isn't about talking louder or faster or being more aggressive. It's about rhythm. Matching tempo, reading cues, being steady when everyone else is rushing or checking out.

That Friday night taught me more than any training ever did. The best opportunities show up when everyone else has quit for the day. People who look tired or blue-collar are often the most ready to buy if someone treats them with respect. One honest question is worth more than ten minutes of a pitch. Silence is where truth lives.

**LESSON IN A BREATH**

*Being easy to buy from means staying calm and present when others quit. Prospects who "don't look like buyers" often are, if someone stops to ask*

Being easy to buy from means staying calm and present when others quit. Prospects who "don't look like buyers" often are, if someone stops to ask

### Endnotes: The Friday Close

[1] Appearance Bias in Sales First impressions and socioeconomic bias affect sales treatment and close rates, filtering out qualified buyers based on appearance rather than readiness. [2] Transaction Ease and Satisfaction Salesforce Consumer Research. Perceived ease of transaction and low-pressure environments produce higher prospect satisfaction and conversion rates across retail and service industries. [3] Late-Day Purchase Intent Late-day and end-of-week prospects demonstrate higher purchase intent when given appropriate attention and respect.

## Clouds and Concrete

Emotionally, it's easier to fall off a cloud than to bounce off concrete.

But when you are living on commission, how do you stay level? Here's how.

I did it. When I was consistent, it worked. 50 percent close rate. Five sales out of ten prospects with an average commission of $300. 10 prospects, five sales, $1,500.

But if I moved one step back... That meant I had ten prospects. On an average week. $1,500 per week. That meant every person who walked through the door was worth $150 to me.

It didn't matter if they bought or not. It didn't matter whether they came in for a brochure ten minutes before closing, sweaty and tired after work. It didn't matter if it was an underage kid who wouldn't be buying a car for another year, and their parents weren't even there, killing time on a Saturday afternoon.

They all became worth $150.

It was simple math, but it changed everything about how I saw people that walked into that showroom.

But that only worked if I stayed in what I started calling my 60/40 balance. Not too high when things went well. Not too low when they didn't. Somewhere in the middle, steady, even when I didn't feel steady inside.

If I celebrated too hard after a good sale, if I let myself get too excited or too confident, my average would plummet. If I fell into frustration after someone walked, if I let that sour feeling sit in my chest and affect how I greeted the next person-same result.

The math didn't work unless I stayed consistent.

So, I kept track of how many people I saw each week. Didn't focus on closes or commission. Counted conversations. And lo and behold, when I kept my energy consistent, the sales stayed consistent too.

In fact, after only two months of this approach, I became salesperson of the month on a floor with fifteen people. Most of them were double my age, with fifteen, twenty, or thirty years of experience. Guys who'd been selling since I was in elementary school.

And I beat them with a notepad and basic emotional control.

I won salesperson of the month consistently for the next three years until I was promoted to sales manager. Not because I was more talented or more charismatic. Because I'd figured out how to stay level. What's interesting is how frustrated the rest of the sales team became during that initial period. We all got along fine, but they continuously teased me about my approach. About how I made stupid jokes when someone came in instead of launching into a pitch. About how I treated tire-kickers the same as serious buyers. They thought I was wasting time.

On Saturdays at noon, when someone showed up holding a bag with lunch, they knew it was for me. Brought by the people I was helping. Prospects who liked me enough to bring me food. The other guys would shake their heads, laugh, and make jokes about it. But those prospects almost always bought from me.

It was incredibly empowering. I had learned something that didn't depend on being naturally gifted or having years of experience.

When you control the emotions, the numbers take care of themselves. Not always immediately. Not always, obviously. But consistently. Over time.

With enough repetition that you trust it even on the days when it feels like nothing's working.

Figure 3: The $150 Prospect Math

**$150 CUSTOMER MATH**

*Every conversation has value*

$150 × 10 = $1,500

per prospect | weekly conversations | predictable weekly value

$150 $150 $150 $150 $150 $150 $150 $150 $150 $150

When every prospect has value, emotional steadiness replaces the sales rollercoaster.

*Figure 3: The $150 Prospect Math*

That $150 prospect taught me more than any sales training ever did. It taught me that everyone has value, even when you can't see it yet. That consistency beats intensity. Your emotional state determines your outcomes more than your skill level does. That you can reverse-engineer success if you're willing to track the right things and trust the process even when it's boring. This was the raw, early form of what would become the Six Laws.

---

**LESSON IN A BREATH**

*Every person has measurable value; emotional steadiness turns potential into predictable results.*

---

Every person has measurable value; emotional steadiness turns potential into predictable results.

## Endnotes: The $150 Prospect

[1] Emotional Regulation and Performance Moderate, consistent emotional states improve decision-making and performance compared to high-variability emotional patterns. [2] Leading Indicators Kaplan, R. S. & Norton, D. P. "The Balanced Scorecard," Harvard Business Review. Process metrics (activity-based) predict outcomes more reliably than result metrics (outcome-based) in sales and performance environments. [3] Systems Over Talent Systematic approaches to prospect interaction reduce dependency on individual talent and create more predictable, scalable results across sales teams. - Equal Treatment and Conversion Value-neutral treatment of prospects reduces cognitive bias in qualification and increases conversion rates across diverse prospect segments. Chapter 2: Control

# Chapter 2: Control (Greenwich Acura, 1995–2002)

(Greenwich Acura, 1995–2002)

I was twenty-seven when they gave me the keys to Greenwich Acura. Not metaphorical keys. Actual keys. Heavy on the ring, cold in my hand on the mornings I needed to unlock the building before anyone else arrived.

Not every morning. The ones that mattered. Days when I knew we had a big delivery coming, or when I needed thirty minutes of silence to think through a problem before the phones started ringing. I learned early that showing up exhausted doesn't make you a better leader. It makes you tired.

The dealership was mine to run. General Manager. It sounded impressive until I stood alone in the empty showroom, realizing that in a few hours this place would be full of people twice my age who'd been selling cars since I was in middle school. People who'd seen managers come and go.

People watched to see if I knew what I was doing. I didn't. Not yet.

At Honda, I'd learned to survive. Figured out how to read people, stay calm when deals fell apart, and keep my rhythm steady. But leading? That was different. Selling is about managing yourself through one interaction at a time. Leadership is about creating conditions where people can succeed simultaneously without everything collapsing into chaos.

The pressure wasn't the hours. It was the choices. Every decision mattered in ways that weren't always obvious until later. Who got which prospect. How we handled a complaint. Whether we answered the phone by the third ring or let it go to voicemail. Small things that added up to culture, to trust, to whether people believed I knew what I was doing.

I made mistakes. Plenty of them.

The loneliest part wasn't the responsibility. It was in realizing that the same energy and instinct that made me good at selling didn't automatically translate to leading. Being liked mattered less. Being clear did. Being steady did. Having a system that worked even on the days when I wasn't at my best.

At Acura, I learned that what you build matters more than how hard you work.

## The GM Breakthrough

General Manager of Greenwich Acura, one of the wealthiest zip codes in

the country. The kind of place where prospects drove in wearing Rolex watches and left in brand-new TLs without blinking at the price.

The team had experience. Confident. Most of them had been selling longer than I'd been alive. They averaged about thirty new cars per month, which sounds decent until you realize the potential sitting in that showroom, in that zip code, with that brand.

I didn't come in trying to be anyone's hero. I came in wanting to understand what was happening. So I listened first.

For two weeks, I watched. Sat in my office with the door open.

I walked the floor. Listened to phone calls. Watched how people moved through the day. And I started noticing things that made little sense.

Phones rang five, six times before anyone answered them. Sometimes seven. Sometimes, nobody picked up at all. When someone finally did answer, the conversation was brief. Controlled. Rigid.

"We don't give prices over the phone." "You need to come in for that." "We require appointments for test drives." The focus was on control. Keep the prospect off balance. Make them come in.

Don't give away information. Force urgency. Classic old-school tactics that probably worked in 1985 but felt wrong in 1995.

Result? Continuous hang-ups. People are calling back and asking for someone else. Lost leads we'd never even know about because they'd move on to the next dealership.

I started tracking it. Of every ten calls, maybe three turned into appointments. And out of those three, maybe one showed up. We were burning through leads like they didn't matter, like there were infinite prospects waiting to be treated like inconveniences.

The team didn't see it as a problem. They saw it as filtering. "If they're not serious enough to come in, they're not real buyers." That's what one of the senior guys told me when I asked about the phone strategy.

But I'd spent five years watching real buyers. I knew what serious looked like. And serious buyers don't enjoy playing games. They want information. They want to feel respected. They want to know you're not going to waste their time or treat them like marks.

So, I rebuilt the system.

I didn't announce it as a big initiative or a new philosophy. I changed the rules quietly, one piece at a time.

We started giving callers a real retail price and a competitive estimate. Not a fake number to get them in the door. The actual price. It opened the conversation instead of ending it.

We invited them to refine the deal in person, but we didn't force urgency. No "this deal expires today" pressure.

Honest information and an invitation to continue the conversation when they were ready.

Everyone got trained to confirm who would make the buying decision. Not in a pushy way. A natural question. "Will anyone else be involved in this decision?" Because there's limited value in building a relationship with someone who can't say yes.

We left pricing discussions for after the test drive, once value was established. Let them fall in love with the car first. Let them see themselves in it. Then talk numbers.

And I introduced one more rule, something I called the Three-Ring Rule.

If a phone rang over three times, I answered it myself. And I didn't pay a salesperson commission.

That got people moving. These small structural shifts would serve as early evidence of what would come later.

Within two months, sales doubled. Same staff. Same inventory. Same showroom. We went from thirty cars a month to sixty. No magic. No heroics. Removing friction and replacing pressure with structure.

The older guys on the team didn't love me for it at first. A few of them thought I was giving away too much information, making it too easy for prospects to shop with us. One guy said, "You're giving the prospect control." But the numbers didn't lie. And when their paychecks started doubling, the complaints stopped.

The owner and controller called and asked what I did to double revenue so quickly. When I told them, their general reaction was, "Well, that's not complicated; we could've done that." But they never seem to, do they?

**LESSON IN A BREATH**

*Structure removes friction; accessibility builds trust faster than any sales tactic ever will.*

Structure removes friction; accessibility builds trust faster than any sales tactic ever will.

### Endnotes: The GM Breakthrough

[1] Response Speed and Abandonment Baymard Institute, Cart Abandonment Research. Each additional ring before answer sharply reduces conversion rates and increases abandonment. [2] Price Transparency and Trust Mohan, B. & Buell, R. "Lifting the Veil: The Benefits of Cost Transparency," Harvard Business School. Transparency in pricing and product information produces higher trust levels and conversion rates in retail environments, particularly for high-involvement purchases. [3] Friction Reduction and Conversion Baymard Institute, Checkout Optimization Research. Process optimization and friction reduction in sales environments improve conversion rates without requiring additional resources or personnel changes. - Structural vs. Individual Interventions Buono, A. F. & Kerber, K. W. "Building Organizational Change Capacity," Research in Organizational Change and Development. Structural changes in prospect interaction protocols produce more sustainable performance improvements than individual skill development or motivational interventions.

## Saturday Operations

Saturdays at Greenwich Acura started at seven-thirty with coffee and a legal pad. I'd get there before the team, before the phones started. By nine o'clock, the day would be chaos if I didn't have a plan.

Saturdays were when most people showed up. Couples, families, comparison shoppers. By ten o'clock, twelve groups on the lot, six salespeople, and me—trying to track who was with whom and what stage each deal was in.

Without structure, it turned into a scramble. Salespeople stepping on each other. Prospects waiting too long. Deals falling apart. So, I started making lists.

Nothing fancy. A legal pad with three columns: Prospect Name, Salesperson, Status. I'd update it every thirty minutes. Walk the floor. Check in. Write down where things stood. If someone was waiting for a manager's approval, I knew it. If a test drive had been out too long, I knew it. If a prospect had been sitting in finance for forty-five minutes, I knew it before they got frustrated enough to leave.

The team thought it was overkill. "You don't trust us?" But it wasn't about trust. It was about visibility.

On a busy Saturday, you can't see everything at once. You can't be in three places at the same time. But you can know what's happening if you're tracking it. And when you know what's happening, you can fix problems before they become losses.

One Saturday, a couple had been waiting on finance for over an hour. Getting quieter, that dangerous kind of quiet.

I pulled the salesperson aside. "Walk them around service. Buy ten minutes." He did. They relaxed. Twenty minutes later, they signed. That's what the list did. It let me see the bottleneck before it killed the deal.

Waiting kills deals. A prospect in finance for forty-five minutes starts second-guessing. Someone standing alone for three minutes walks out. I tracked wait times to the minute.

The team thought I was obsessive. "People understand it takes time." But most prospects won't tell you they're frustrated. They'll leave.

I started teaching the team to recognize dead time. If a prospect was waiting on something they could not control, do not let them sit there.

Paperwork, an approval, a manager's signature. Engage them. Don't let them sit there. Keep the relationship alive.

By mid-afternoon on busy Saturdays, I'd learned to read the energy of the entire floor by looking at my legal pad and watching how long people had been in each stage. If I saw three deals stuck in the same stage, I knew where the problem was. If I saw a salesperson with two active prospects at once, I knew he needed help. If I saw someone who had written nothing down in two hours, I knew they were either losing deals or not writing them down, and either way, I needed to check.

The structure didn't make Saturdays easy. It made them manageable.

I wasn't trying to control every conversation or micromanage every move. I tried to create a system where everyone could do their job without tripping over each other or losing track of what mattered. And what mattered was simple: keep deals moving, keep prospects engaged, don't let anything sit too long.

The older salespeople eventually stopped complaining about the list. A few of them started asking me to check it when they couldn't find a manager or needed to know if finance was available. It became part of how we worked.

By my second year as GM, the team had internalized the flow principle.

I'd see salespeople walking prospects out to look at other models while they waited for finance. I'd see them offering coffee, showing them the service department, talking about anything other than the deal that was currently stuck.

And our close rate went up. Not because we got better at selling.

Because we got better at preventing people from getting lost during the wait.

One of the veteran guys told me, "You know what the difference is here versus other places I've worked? We don't let deals die of boredom." That was it exactly. Deals die of boredom. They die in the gaps. They die when prospects have too much time to think about all the reasons they shouldn't buy.

Deals die of boredom.

If you keep them engaged, if you keep things moving, they stay in the moment. And the moment is where decisions happen.

I went home most Saturdays around six or seven. Tired, but not destroyed. The structure gave me a way to stay ahead of the chaos without living in it.

---

**LESSON IN A BREATH**

*Structure creates visibility; managing wait time keeps deals alive during inevitable delays.*

---

Structure creates visibility; managing wait time keeps deals alive during inevitable delays.

### Endnotes: Saturday Operations

[1] Systematic Tracking in High-Volume Environments High-volume service environments require systematic tracking mechanisms to prevent prospect abandonment and maintain service quality during peak periods. [2] Leadership Visibility and Proactive Problem-Solving Information visibility in leadership contexts enables proactive problem-solving and reduces reactive crisis management in complex operational environments. [3] Wait-Time Perception and Purchase Completion Prospect wait-time perception impacts satisfaction and purchase completion rates, with negative effects compounding after

threshold durations. - Proactive Communication During Delays Proactive communication during service delays reduces prospect frustration and abandonment compared to passive waiting environments. - Engagement During Wait Periods Psychological engagement activities during unavoidable wait periods maintain positive emotional states and reduce perceived time duration.

## Preparation and Integration

I started keeping a notebook—not a to-do list—a sequence. If we had deliveries on Tuesday morning, I'd write down everything that needed to happen beforehand. Keys ready. Paperwork staged. Salespeople briefed.

I called it stacking. Sequencing predictable tasks the night before so I could think instead of react.

One Monday, I looked at Tuesday's chaos: three deliveries, two test drives, regional visit at two. I made a list for the team. By eleven, everything was done. Nobody panicked. Nobody scrambled.

But one problem kept recurring: sales and service didn't talk. Sales scheduled deliveries without checking with the service department. Prospects showed up to dirty cars.

So, I started showing up for service every morning. Five minutes. To communicate. After two weeks, the service manager started asking about the schedule before I got there.

They scheduled three deliveries for Saturday on Thursday, but the service department was packed. Old system: I'd find out Saturday afternoon. New system: I had the salespeople call the prospects, offer choices, and move two to Monday. No fires.

I had the salespeople walk prospects through service before they left. Introduced them to the manager. Showed them where to pull in. First visits for service jumped. Return sales increased.

Fifteen minutes every night. Look at tomorrow, identify gaps, and communicate with the service. I stopped feeling constantly behind. I went home knowing tomorrow was half handled.

---

**LESSON IN A BREATH**

*Advance preparation eliminates predictable fires; daily communication prevents departmental gaps from becoming prospect problems.*

---

Advance preparation eliminates predictable fires; daily communication prevents departmental gaps from becoming prospect problems.

## Team Dynamics

The first time I called a team meeting as GM, three guys didn't show up.

Not because they forgot. They didn't think they needed to be there. They'd been selling cars for twenty years. What was a twenty-seven-year-old kid going to teach them?

I didn't make a big deal of it. Didn't call them out. Didn't threaten anything. But I noticed. And they knew I noticed.

The dynamics were clear from day one. I was young. They were experienced. Some of them had been at this dealership longer than I'd been driving. They were polite, mostly. But there was a test happening. With every decision I made, they watched to see if I knew what I was doing. You can't lead people who don't respect you by demanding respect. You earn it by being consistent, by making good calls, and by not pretending to know things you don't.

One afternoon, an experienced salesperson named Tom came into my office. He'd been selling for thirty years, had his own way of doing everything, and wasn't shy about telling you when he thought you were wrong.

He wanted to close a deal his way. It involved a pricing structure that technically violated our agreement with Acura. Not by much. Enough to cause problems if corporate found out.

I said no.

He pushed back. "I've been doing this since before you went to high school. This is how deals get done." I didn't argue with his experience. I said, "I believe you. But if this deal blows back on us, it's my name on it. And I can't risk the dealership over one sale." He wasn't happy. Walked out, shaking his head. But he didn't do the deal.

Two weeks later, another dealership got flagged by Acura for the same pricing issue. Tom heard about it. Came into my office, said nothing, nodded once, and walked out.

After that, he stopped testing me.

The team wasn't a problem to solve. They needed to see that I would not make that decision out of ego or insecurity. That I would not pretend I knew everything. That I would listen to their experience but still make the last call when it mattered.

Every Monday morning, I'd spend fifteen minutes walking the floor and talking. Not a formal meeting. Presence. When someone needed help later in the week, they came to me because I'd already shown up for them. Richard, a seasoned salesperson at Greenwich Acura for twelve years, pulled me aside one Saturday. We were slammed. He had two prospects, both serious, both ready to buy, and he couldn't handle both at once.

He said, "I need help. Can you take one?" He didn't ask because he had to. He asked because he trusted me to get the deal done.

I took the second prospect. Test drive. Numbers. Closed the deal. Later, he said, "You're okay." That was it. Acknowledgment.

Leading experienced people isn't about proving you're smarter or more talented. It's about showing you're steady. That you won't panic when things get hard. That you'll make the tough calls when needed. That you respect what they know but won't let the team drift into bad habits because "that's how we've always done it." They didn't need me to teach them how to sell. They needed me to create an environment where they could do their jobs without unnecessary chaos, poor decisions from above, or a GM who thought he had all the answers.

By the end of my first year, the guys who skipped that first meeting were showing up early. Not because I demanded it. They wanted to know what was happening. They trusted that if I was calling a meeting, it mattered.

That's what respect looks like. It's quiet. It's earned. And you can tell when the team shows up.

---

**LESSON IN A BREATH**

*You can't demand respect from experienced people; you earn it through steady decisions.*

---

You can't demand respect from experienced people; you earn it through steady decisions.

## Early Leadership Lessons

I fired someone for the first time on a Wednesday afternoon in October.

He was late three times in two weeks. Not massively late. Fifteen, twenty minutes. But late enough that other people noticed. And when others notice, it becomes a problem, even if the work is getting done.

I'd talked to him twice already. Friendly warnings. "Hey, we need you here on time. The team's counting on you." He'd nod, say he understood, then show up late again the following week.

The third time, I knew what I had to do. But I didn't want to do it.

I was 28 years old, and I'd never fired anyone. I'd seen managers do it. Watched them walk someone to the door. But doing it yourself is different. You're ending someone's income. Their routine. Maybe putting stress on their family. I spent the entire morning dreading it. Kept finding reasons to put it off. Finally, at around three o'clock, I called him into my office.

I didn't drag it out. Told him it wasn't working. Gave him his last check. He didn't argue. Nodded, cleaned out his desk, and left.

The whole thing took maybe ten minutes.

What surprised me was what happened after. I expected the team to be uncomfortable. Maybe resentful. Instead, two people came into my office separately that afternoon and said the same thing: "Thanks for handling that." Turns out, everyone knew he was a problem. His lateness was creating extra work for other people. They were covering for him. Resenting him. Waiting to see if I'd do anything about it.

Being liked isn't leadership. Making the hard call when it's needed is leadership. And sometimes the team respects you more for doing the uncomfortable thing than for being nice. Another lesson came about six months later.

We were having a rough month. Sales were down. Not catastrophically, but enough that tension rose. I called a team meeting on a Monday morning. My plan was to give a motivational speech. Rally the troops. Get everyone fired up.

I stood at the front of the room and talked about effort, attitude, and pushing through a slump. Standard manager stuff.

About three minutes in, I could see it. People weren't buying it. Their eyes glazed over while they nodded politely. I was losing them.

So, I stopped mid-sentence.

I said, "You know what? This isn't helpful. You all know we're down. Telling you to try harder will not fix it." The room got quiet. Everyone looked at me.

I said, "Here's what I think. The market's slow right now. That's not your fault. But we can control how we handle the phones. We can control follow-up. We can control whether we're talking to prospects who came in two weeks ago and didn't buy." Then I asked, "What's one thing we're not doing well right now that we could fix?" Someone in the back said, "We're not calling people back fast enough." Someone else said, "We've got fifteen people on our follow-up list that nobody's touched in a month." The meeting turned into a working session. We made a list. Assigned responsibilities. Set a goal for the week.

That week, we closed four deals from old leads. Not because of motivation. Because we did the work. Teams don't need inspirational speeches. They need obvious problems and a plan to solve them. They need a leader who's honest about what's not working instead of pretending everything's fine.

The hardest lesson came during my second year. I made a bad hire. Knew within two weeks it would not work. But I waited three months, telling myself he needed time to adjust. By the time I finally let him go, the damage had spread to the whole team. One of the veterans told me afterward, "I think you waited too long on that one." He was right. Waiting does not make hard decisions easier. It makes the damage worse.

**LESSON IN A BREATH**

*Leadership is choosing clarity over comfort in small, uncomfortable decisions that matter.*

Leadership is choosing clarity over comfort in small, uncomfortable decisions that matter.

## The Box (From Operations to Closes)

I sat in my office on a Tuesday morning, staring at a list of twenty-three things that needed my attention, and I did not know which one to do first.

A salesperson needed manager approval on a deal. Service had a prospect complaint I needed to handle. Finance was waiting for a signature. The corporation wanted the monthly report by the end of the day. The sales manager needed to talk about next week's schedule. And I had three voicemails I hadn't returned yet.

Everything felt urgent. Everything felt important. And I couldn't decide where to start.

This wasn't new. It had been building for weeks. The dealership ran better, but I was drowning. Every time I focused on one area, three others caught fire.

I was reactive, and it was exhausting.

That Tuesday morning, something shifted. Maybe it was frustration. Maybe I was tired of feeling behind. But I grabbed a blank sheet of paper and drew a box, a simple box. Four squares.

I didn't know what I was doing yet. I needed to see everything at once instead of letting it pile up in my head.

I labeled the first square: Value. What moves the business forward?

The second square: Need. What must happen today, no matter what?

The third square: Decision Makers. What requires my approval or input that no one else can provide?

The fourth square: Affordability. What can wait, or what can someone else handle?

The Box wasn't about productivity or time management. It was about clarity.

When everything feels urgent, nothing gets the attention it deserves.

When you separate what's most important from what feels loud, you can work on the right things in the right order.

## Moving the Box to the Close

The Prerequisite: Like → Trust → Understand It occurred to me that what worked for the organization could also help a prospect organize their concerns.

Before you ever enter The Box, you must earn the right to have that conversation. The order is not optional: Like → Trust → Understand. If they do not feel comfortable with you, they will not open up. If they do not trust you, they will not tell you the truth. And if they do not understand the product, they cannot decide, no matter how good the offer is. Most failed closes are not closing issues; they are missing steps in this order. The Box only works when you have put in the time up front and earned the clarity needed for an honest, pressure-free conversation.

## The Four Squares

Value Do they believe this product or service is better than what they are doing now or another option? Prospects do not compare prices first; they compare confidence. Value is clarity that the new direction is genuinely better than the current one or alternatives.

Too far – you are not worth the extra distance Too expensive – I got a better price, or I believe another brand gives me more for less Need Is this a want or is it time? A prospect can love the idea and still hesitate because they have not connected the decision to a necessary change in their life. Need is emotional, not logical.

My job is okay for now – I want to make a change, but I do not need to My computer still works well enough – this is not an essential purchase I can survive on another staycation – I cannot prioritize travel Decision Makers Are the right people in the conversation? If someone else's voice matters, momentum stalls until that person is part of the decision. Spouse, boss, partner, manager Affordability They want it, believe in it, and understand it, but need to fit it into their real life. If it is a want, it will not be prioritized. If needed, they will work with you.

If you focus on affordability before closing the other three boxes first, you will struggle.

The Box is not a script. It is a moment of honesty.

Step 1: Ask open-ended questions designed to isolate challenges For example: Are there any other products or services you are considering? How do you feel they compare to my product?

What is the most important thing in your decision?

Where does this fit on your priority list?

Do you have someone or people you count on for advice or agreement when making important decisions?

Most prospects tell you immediately.

People know what is holding them back; they do not know how to say it.

When you give them the language, they give you the truth.

Step 2: Actively listen and rephrase the answers in a simple one-or two-sentence reply For example: "I think what you are saying is there are other options that you feel might have better VALUE, is that right?" Put them in the figurative box.

Step 3: Ask them what they like about your service or product and let them tell you, not the other way around Most times they will solve things for themselves if you have established like, trust, and understanding.

One afternoon at the Bloomfield campus, a prospect named John sat across from me. Arms crossed. He said, "There are schools closer to home." I did not counter. I said, "So it sounds like it is not whether this works. It is whether the distance is worth it. Is that right?" He nodded.

"What made you drive out here in the first place?" He listed three things. Hands-on training. Certifications. Job placement. I let him sit with that for a second.

"So it is not the distance. It is the value." He said, "Yeah. I guess it is." That was the Box. I did not sell him anything. I gave him the language for what was already in his head. He moved himself from hesitation to clarity. A week later, different prospect, different campus. A couple sat together. She said, "We love the idea. Just not sure it is the right time." I said, "So it is not the program. It is timing. Is that fair?" "Yes." "If nothing changed between now and next year, would waiting help, or would starting now get you there sooner?" She looked at her husband. He looked at her. She said, "Starting now." Same tool. Different square. She was not stuck on value. She was stuck on need. Once I named it, she solved it herself.

## Why The Box Works

The Box removes pressure.

It removes guessing.

It removes heroic selling.

It gives people the space to think clearly.

When clarity rises, movement follows.

---

**LESSON IN A BREATH**

*Clarity moves people forward. Pressure pushes them away.*

---

Clarity moves people forward. Pressure pushes them away.

## The First Collapse

By the end of my second year as GM, things were clicking. Sales were up. The team was solid. Saturdays ran smoothly. The Box kept me from drowning. I had figured out how to lead without burning out. Confidence came.

That is when I stopped doing the things that got me there.

It happened gradually. A Friday here and there, where I skipped the Saturday Stack. A Tuesday when I didn't draw The Box. Small shortcuts that didn't seem to matter.

For a few weeks, it was fine. We were still running well. The momentum from months of structure carried us. I started thinking maybe I did not need the systems as much as I thought. Maybe I had gotten better at this. Maybe I could trust my instincts more and rely on preparation less. That is the thing about overconfidence. It feels like growth. It feels like you have leveled up. You are ignoring the foundation that is holding everything together.

It started cracking in March.

We had a big month planned. The corporation ran a sales incentive. We had inventory coming in. We scheduled some regional advertising. Everything was set up for us to have our best month of the year.

I did not prep as I normally would. Did not sit down Sunday night and map out the month. Did not check in with service about capacity. Did not make sure finance was ready for volume. I assumed it would work out because it had been working out.

The first week was fine. In the second week, things started slipping. A delivery got delayed because service was backed up, and nobody had flagged it. A prospect waited two hours in finance because we did not have enough staff scheduled to handle the volume. A salesperson missed a follow-up call because I had not checked the list in three days.

Small things. Individually, they did not kill us. But they added up.

By the third week, I could feel it. The team grew frustrated. Prospects were less happy. Deals were taking longer to close. The energy that had been building all year was souring.

One Thursday afternoon, the owner came into my office and closed the door. That is never good.

He said, "What is going on? We have been solid for months. Now everything feels chaotic again." I did not have a good answer. I knew what was going on. I had stopped doing the work. But I did not want to admit it. So I said something about it being a busy month and that we would get through it.

He looked at me for a second, then said, "We've had busy months before. This feels different." He was right. It felt different. Because we had lost the discipline.

That night, I stayed late. Not to catch up on work. To think. I pulled out my notebook. Looked at the last few weeks. All the small things I had stopped doing. The Saturday Stack I had skipped. The Box I had not drawn. The daily check-ins with service I had let slide because I was "too busy." I had gotten comfortable. And comfort, I was learning, is where discipline dies.

Comfort is where discipline dies.

Hero systems fail quietly long before they fail publicly.

The next morning, I got there early. Drew The Box. Made the list. Walked back to service and checked their schedule. Pulled the sales manager aside and asked him to help me get back on track. He said, "You need to do Friday prep again. That is when things started slipping." I said, "I know. I stopped doing it because I thought we did not need it anymore." He shook his head. "We need it more now than we did when we started. We are busier. There is more to track." He was right.

It took two weeks to stabilize. Two weeks of going back to basics. Saturday Stack every Friday. Box every morning. Daily service check-ins. Tracking the floor. Following up on deals. All the things that felt boring and repetitive, but kept everything from falling apart.

By the end of March, we were back. Not at our best, but functional. We hit our sales goal for the month, barely. But it felt hollow because I knew we could have crushed it if I had not gotten lazy.

One of the veteran salespeople pulled me aside at the end of the month. He said, "You alright? You were off for a few weeks there." I said, "Yeah. I stopped doing the things that had been working. Will not happen again." He nodded. "Good. Because when you are off, we all feel it." That hit me. I had been thinking about my systems as personal tools. Things that helped me stay organized. But they were not for me. They were for the entire team. When I stopped using them, everyone suffered.

The First Collapse was not dramatic. We did not lose a ton of money. Nobody quit. No major disasters. It was a slow degradation. A loss of sharpness. A return to chaos that I thought we had left behind.

But it taught me something I would never forget: systems are not training wheels you remove once you are confident. They are the foundation. The better you get, the more you need them. The better you get, the more complexity you are managing. And complexity without structure is chaos waiting to happen. Confidence without discipline is dangerous. It makes you think you have outgrown the basics and forgotten why they added up.

After that month, I never skipped the Saturday Stack again. Never went a day without The Box. Never let a week go by without checking in on the things that kept us stable.

Not because I was scared. Because I had learned that maintaining good systems is easier than rebuilding them after they collapse.

The best leaders are not the ones who never make mistakes. They are the ones who recognize the collapse before it destroys everything, and they have the discipline to go back to what works.

That March taught me: structure is not optional. It is not something you do until you are good enough to stop. It is what allows you to stay good.

---

**LESSON IN A BREATH**

*Systems are not training wheels; they are the foundation that enables you to handle greater complexity.*

---

Systems are not training wheels; they are the foundation that enables you to handle greater complexity.

This failure plants the seed of Law 6: Collapse, systems drift quietly before they break loudly. Chapter 3: Discovery

# Chapter 3: Discovery (DirectBuy, 2002–2012)

(DirectBuy, 2002–2012)

When I left Greenwich Acura, I thought I understood rhythm. Tight process. Small team. Predictable flow. DirectBuy ripped that open. It showed me what happens when the environment changes, but the human patterns underneath stay exactly the same.

To even qualify for a DirectBuy franchise, you had to complete six weeks of training. Half of it was pure sales mechanics. Three straight weeks of scripts, cadence, presentation order, and process steps. They scripted everything from greeting to close. It felt like buying a system out of a box.

And surprisingly… it worked.

But the more I watched, the more one thing kept jumping out. In this model, the salesperson did everything. They called customers, answered their calls, greeted them, got to know them, gave a long presentation, and made the sale. It was one person trying to run an entire assembly line.

And this was the first time I saw the pattern clearly. When one person owns the entire rhythm, the rhythm eventually collapses. Not because the person is bad. Because no human can keep a perfect pace across every stage indefinitely. I started working with the Vice President of Sales at the corporate level, and together we began shifting the model. Instead of one person grinding through every step, we separated the labor into distinct rhythms. Call center agents who only made calls. Salespeople who only presented. Each part had its own lane. Each lane had its own tempo.

Within a short period, we opened three locations with 20 salespeople and 30 call center agents. Same scripts. Same process. But we divided the rhythm correctly, so the system scaled.

These patterns weren't Honda patterns or Acura patterns. They were human patterns. And human patterns travel.

## The Call Room

The problem was obvious by the end of month one. The salespeople burned out before prospects even walked in.

They'd spend the morning hammering outbound calls. Two hundred dials a week, hoping for eight appointments. By the time someone showed up for a ninety-minute presentation, they were exhausted. Exhausted salespeople can't build the energy needed for a big decision.

DirectBuy wasn't like Acura. The product was a membership, not a car. The sales cycle was educational, not impulse-driven. Prospects came for a structured presentation and then decided whether to join. That presentation required sharpness, patience, and emotional capacity.

But the system forced one person to do everything. Make the calls. Take the inbound calls. Greet at the door. Build a connection. Deliver the presentation. Close the deal.

One person trying to run an assembly line alone. And no matter how talented they were, the rhythm collapsed.

The pattern became obvious in week three. The salespeople who made the most calls in the morning gave the weakest presentations in the afternoon. Those who saved energy for presentations didn't make enough calls to keep their pipelines alive. It was an impossible tradeoff.

The math wasn't the problem. The rhythm was the problem.

I called other franchise owners. Most were experiencing the same collapse. Some tried hiring more salespeople, but that added more people to a broken process.

Then I talked to the VP of Sales. We thought the same thing.

"What if we split it?

Call center agents make the calls, and salespeople only handle the in-person presentation and close." It felt risky. DirectBuy built its entire philosophy on one person's ownership of the relationship. Splitting roles meant trusting a handoff. And handoffs can kill deals if you aren't careful.

But the current system was killing people.

So we tested it. The VP of Sales had been watching the same patterns I had. He would float ideas, small adjustments to the call flow, timing changes, ways to reduce friction before the appointment. I tested them at the franchise level. Some worked. Some didn't. But he paid attention to the results.

When I brought the call center concept to him, the seasoned trainers pushed back hard. He didn't. He said, "Test it. If the numbers move, we expand it." That backing mattered. I was not a lone voice fighting the system. Someone inside the organization had seen the same cracks and was willing to let me swing at them.

We built a call room. Five desks. Five phones. Agents whose sole job was outbound rhythm. Follow the script. Follow the cadence. Book the appointment. Their job was to surface interest, not solve objections. When hesitation appeared, they weren't diagnosing which square it lived in, that was the closer's job. The division was instinctive. No pressure to close. No improvising. No heroics.

Once the appointment arrived, the sales team took over. Fresh. Focused. Ready.

And it worked instantly. The call agents stayed in rhythm because their job was simple. The salespeople stayed sharp because they didn't exhaust themselves before the show. And the appointments were higher quality because they came from consistent touchpoints instead of sporadic bursts of effort.

Within two months, presentations jumped. Close rates increased. All with the same team. Same scripts. Same training. Divided rhythm. The principle underneath: you had to give people a sustainable role before you could ask them to sustain performance.

Some salespeople resisted. They felt like they were losing control.

"What if the agent sets it wrong?" "What if they can't answer a question?" Easy.

"They don't answer it. They say, 'Our specialist will go through that with you when you come in.'" No improvising. No personal flair. Rhythm.

Eventually, the results silenced the resistance.

The call room became the engine. The sales floor became the closer. Each part had its lane. Each lane had its tempo. And for the first time, I saw a system scale beyond individual talent.

Because it wasn't dependent on the hero. It depended on the rhythm. The system gave before it asked. It served salespeople by protecting their energy so they could better serve prospects. I didn't call it Reciprocity yet, but the pattern was unmistakable.

## The System Without Me

Three days out of town. That's all it took. I expected chaos when I returned. Questions. Delayed decisions. Deals that needed rescuing. Instead, I walked into a perfectly normal Tuesday. Phones humming. Appointments set. Presentations running.

Nobody noticed I'd been gone.

I checked the numbers. Calls steady. Appointments steady. Guests steady. Closes steady.

It took me a minute to process what I was seeing.

This was the first time I'd ever built a system that didn't require my presence. At Acura, the systems worked because I was the one directing the rhythm. I was the hub.

At DirectBuy... I wasn't the hub. The process was the hub.

That changed everything.

If the system ran without me for three days, it could run without me for a week. If it could run in Queens and Manhattan while I was in Boston, it could run in all three at once. If it didn't need my instincts, it didn't need my personality or my improvisation. It only needed people willing to follow the rhythm.

I tested it. Stayed out of Queens deliberately. Results held.

I pushed control back to the process rather than to me. Results held.

One day, a salesperson called: "Prospect wants a payment plan we rarely offer. Can I do it?" Old me: "Let me think." New me: "What does the script say?" He checked. "We offer three standard options." "Then the answer is no. Stick to the three." Ten minutes later, he called back.

"They took option two." The system worked because it was simple. No improvising. No special deals. No custom solutions. Standardized rhythm.

When you remove variables, you remove chaos.

When you remove chaos, people no longer need a hero.

By the end of the year, we ran three locations. Twenty salespeople. Thirty call agents. I couldn't physically be everywhere. I didn't need to be.

A system that didn't need me. That was the breakthrough.

---

**LESSON IN A BREATH**

*Systems scale when you divide labor into distinct rhythms, not when you add capacity to chaos.*

---

Systems scale when you divide labor into distinct rhythms, not when you add capacity to chaos.

This structure embodies Law 3: Rhythm, dividing labor into distinct cadences, scales what one person cannot.

## The Presentation Flow

The DirectBuy presentation lasted 90 minutes. Every minute was

scripted. Greeting, introduction, wholesale explanation, product tour, pricing reveal, membership options, close. The training manual spelled out exactly what to say, when to say it, and how long each section should take.

It worked. But it felt mechanical. Prospects sat through it like they watched a lecture, not having a conversation. By minute sixty, you could see some of them checking out. Shifting in their seats. Looking at their watches. And when people check out mentally, they don't buy.

The presentation had been the same for years. Probably decades. Nobody questioned it because it produced results. But I kept thinking: because it works doesn't mean it can't work better.

With corporate executive approval, I started testing minor changes.

Nothing dramatic. Adjustments to the flow.

Instead of front-loading all the explanation, I'd show them something first. Walk them into the showroom where the product samples were displayed. Let them see and touch things before I explained how it all worked. Give them something tangible before hitting them with information.

Instead of following the exact script word-for-word, I'd adjust the pacing based on how engaged they seemed. If they asked questions, I'd slow down and let them talk. If they were bored, I'd speed up and move to the next section. Instead of the rigid seating arrangement the manual recommended, I'd pay attention to how couples naturally positioned themselves and adjust accordingly. Some couples wanted to sit next to each other. Others wanted space. Some needed the husband facing me. Some needed the wife in the lead position. Small things, but they mattered.

The results started improving. Not massively. But consistently. Close rates went from maybe forty-five percent to fifty percent over a few months.

Corporate trainers noticed. And they hated it. I was deviating from the training manual. But I wasn't guessing. I was testing. Tracking. And the numbers backed every change.

I kept adjusting. Quietly. Didn't advertise it. Kept testing and refining based on what worked.

Nothing revolutionary. Modernization.

We tightened the timing. Instead of ninety minutes, we got it down to seventy-five without cutting content. Removed the repetition and the dead air. People appreciated that. Nobody wants to sit through a ninety-minute presentation when seventy-five minutes covers the same ground.

We refined the pricing reveal. Instead of building suspense and dropping all the numbers at once, we walked them through it step by step. Gave them space to think instead of overwhelming them with information all at once.

The sales team noticed the difference. One of them said, "It feels more like a conversation now. Less like we're performing a script." I said, "You're still following the script. You're making it feel natural." He said, "Yeah, but it's easier. Prospects relax more. They ask better questions. It doesn't feel like I'm trying to convince them. It feels like I'm helping them decide." That's exactly what I wanted. The system should feel like guidance, not pressure. Structure, not rigidity. By the end of the year, our close rate was consistently above forty-five percent. Many other franchises were averaging in the thirties. Corporate trainers still didn't love what we were doing, but they couldn't argue with the results.

A few other owners started asking what we'd changed. I walked them through it. Most of them tried a version. Some of them improved. A few went back to the original system because change felt risky.

The best systems aren't the ones that never change. They're the ones that develop based on real feedback while maintaining their core structure. You keep the bones. You refine the execution.

DirectBuy taught me that. The bones were solid. Appointment setting, greeting, preparing the mind, tour with pricing, and close. That sequence worked. But how you moved through it, how you adjusted to the people in front of you, that's where the art lived inside the science.

**LESSON IN A BREATH**

*Systems work best when structure guides the flow, not when rigidity replaces human adaptation.*

Systems work best when structure guides the flow, not when rigidity replaces human adaptation.

## Pattern Recognition

One afternoon, I was visiting the Manhattan location and watching one of

our newer salespeople struggle through a close. He was smart.

Articulate. Knew the product cold. But he was losing the room.

I could see it. The couple was checking out. The husband kept looking at his phone. The wife was staring at the wall. They were done, but the salesperson kept talking. Kept trying to convince them. Kept pushing information. After they left without joining, I pulled him aside. "What happened?" He said, "I don't know. I covered everything. They were interested at first." I said, "They were interested at first. Then you lost them. You saw them disengage, and you kept pushing. That's when it fell apart." He frowned. "What should I have done?" I said, "When someone checks out, you don't give them more information. You give them space. You slow down. You ask a question. You let them re-engage on their terms." He said, "That's not in the script." I said, "The script gets you through the structure. But reading the room keeps them with you."

**LESSON IN A BREATH**

*Patterns discovered in one context reveal themselves everywhere once you know what to watch for. Chapter 4: Expansion*

Patterns discovered in one context reveal themselves everywhere once you know what to watch for. Chapter 4: Expansion

# Chapter 4: Expansion (ICE, 2012–2021)

(International Cruise & Excursions, 2012–2019)

When I joined International Cruise & Excursions. The company was established and profitable, selling shore excursions to cruise passengers and providing white-label services and websites for cruises, resorts, and hotels to big-name companies. I came in to help expand the division: a direct sales vacation club that layered in cruises, hotels, and resorts at significant discounts for members.

Everything looked good on paper. We had a partnership with one of the biggest national retail chains in the country.

The marketing model was simple: set up a kiosk near the checkout line, offer a "free giveaway," collect names and numbers, and hand them off to the call center to book travel presentations later.

It should have been easy money.

Instead, it was chaos in khakis. Shoppers were avoiding eye contact like we were handing out subpoenas.

We'd smile; they'd look away. We'd say hello, they'd speed up. We'd hold out a clipboard, they'd suddenly remember something on the other side of the store.

The worst part? We'd still get leads. People would fill out the forms, out of politeness, out of guilt, out of whatever, but they'd use fake numbers or never answer when we called. And the ones who did answer? They'd say they didn't remember signing up or thought it was for something else entirely. We'd get plenty of "leads", the kind you collect out of politeness, but no one was showing up for the presentations. The conversion rate from clipboard to commitment was flat.

Everyone blamed "the list." The team would say, "These people aren't real leads." Management would say, "We need better locations." The call center would say, "The data's bad." Everybody had an excuse.

I didn't buy it. It wasn't a list problem. It was a sequence problem. Later, I would recognize that broken order as the core mistake Law 5 fixes.

## The Wrong Order

We asked before we gave. Pressuring before we served. Talking

before we listened.

The Reciprocity Sequence. You can't ask first and serve later; that sequence breaks trust. This is Law 5.

Think about it from the prospect's perspective. You're walking through a store trying to grab milk and get home. Some stranger in a polo shirt steps in front of you with a clipboard and a smile that's trying too hard.

"Hey! Quick question, do you like to travel?" Of course you like to travel. Everybody likes to travel. But that's not what they're asking. What they're asking is: "Will you give me your personal information so I can call you later and try to sell you something?" And your limbic brain knows that. So, you say no. Or you lie. Or you give a fake number. Because the whole interaction feels like a trap.

We weren't building trust; we were burning it. I did not have the language yet, but this was my first large-scale lesson in giving before asking. It must come before any serious ask.

## The In-Store Experiment

That morning, I gathered everyone at the kiosk before the store opened. Some looked curious. Most frowned and exchanged glances.

I said, "Today, we're going to act like the best service team this store never hired." They looked at me like I'd started speaking Icelandic.

One guy, Mike, I think his name was, raised his hand. "So, what do we do?" I told them, "If someone looks lost, walk them to the aisle. If they're holding something heavy, carry it. If they ask a question, answer it. And if they clearly don't want help, smile, step aside, and wish them a great day." "That's it?" someone asked.

"That's it." "What about the leads?" "We'll get to that. Trust me." That was the whole playbook. No tablets. No surveys. No giveaways. No "two-minute sweepstakes."

## The Shift

At first, it felt ridiculous, like sending firefighters to hand out

garden hoses. We stood around helping people find cereal and carrying bags of dog food to their cars. No clipboards. No pitches.

Helping. It was the simplest, clearest expression of what I had ever run at scale.

One rep came up to me after the first hour. "I feel useless," she said.

"You're not," I told her. "Keep going." But within that first day, something shifted.

A woman tried to reach something on the top shelf. One of our reps saw her, walked over, and grabbed it for her. The woman smiled and said thank you. That was it. No pitch. No follow-up. A small moment.

Twenty minutes later, that same woman walked by our kiosk and waved. "Thanks again!" she said.

By lunch, eye contact returned; by day two, store employees routed shoppers to us; by day three, the kiosk functioned like a help desk. And here's the thing: we weren't pretending. We liked helping people. It felt good. The work got lighter. The days went faster. The team stopped dreading their shifts.

## Earning the Ask

Only then did we ask again. But now the questions sounded

different.

We'd have a conversation first. We'd help someone find something or answer a question. We'd build a little rapport.

And then, naturally, we'd say: "Quick one, do you and your family like to travel?" If they said yes, we'd add, "We do short, no-pressure presentations that show how to travel for less. It's kind of fun. If it's not for you, no problem. Want me to put your name down?" No tricks.

No urgency traps.

No "you've been selected" nonsense. An invitation, after we'd earned it.

The change was instant and obvious.

When conversations lasted more than a minute, they turned into genuine opportunities.

Better yet, the quality changed.

These weren't polite-lie leads anymore. These were people who wanted to hear what we had to say. They showed up for the presentations.

They brought their spouses. They asked real questions.

Show-to-sale improved. Cancellations dropped. The call center stopped complaining about bad data because the data wasn't bad anymore. But the actual surprise came before the numbers: morale.

Serving people made us calmer, lighter, and prouder of the work. The same reps who'd once sounded pushy now sounded grounded. Their tone changed because their confidence changed, and their confidence changed because their intent did.

Prospects hear intent before they hear words.

We stopped trying to get something from people. We started trying to help them. And once we did that, they wanted to help us back. That's reciprocity. It was the only approach that felt honest and effective.

## The Psychology of Give First

When you give something real, demanding nothing back, people

feel an urge to even the ledger, not out of guilt, but out of balance.

The exchange becomes emotional rather than transactional.

Help flips the threat switch to the trust switch. Threat scans for exits, trust scans for next steps.

It's hard-wired. Someone does you a favor; you want to return the favor. Not because you owe them, but because that's how relationships work. That's how trust builds.

Most salespeople chase obligation. They give you something small, a pen, a free trial, a coffee mug, and then immediately ask for something big in return. That's not reciprocity. That's a trade. And people can smell it.

You give without asking. You help without pitching. You serve without expecting. And then, when you ask, it doesn't feel like pressure. It feels like the natural next step.

I saw it play out repeatedly at those kiosks. A rep would help someone load groceries into their car. The person would thank them. The rep would say, "No problem, have a great day." And then the person would stop and say, "Wait, what is it you guys do here anyway?" That's the moment. That's when the door opens. Not because you forced it. Because they opened it.

When I started, it was one location with four marketing store partners.

A concept that had promise but hadn't exploded yet. Over the next several years, I built it to eight sales centers and twenty-eight marketing partners across different markets. Two in Long Island, two in New Jersey, one in Pennsylvania, one in Arizona, two in California.

Coast to coast.

For the first time, I'd built something from the ground up. At Honda, I was learning to sell. At Acura, I was building systems for one dealership. At DirectBuy, I was scaling three franchises using the same model. But this was different. I wasn't replicating an existing operation. I was building a new division and expanding it across geography, across teams I had to hire and train, across markets that each had its own dynamics.

The challenge wasn't proving the concept. It was maintaining consistency as we grew. When you're running one location, you can see everything. At eight sales centers and twenty-eight partners across multiple states, you can't. You have to create frameworks that hold at a distance. Structures clear enough that a leader three states away can make the same decision you would make.

International Cruise & Excursions exposed every assumption I had about building at distance. Expansion isn't about doing the same thing in more places. It's about building clarity that survives distance. And adaptation only works when the foundation doesn't need you to hold it together.

## Coaching Leaders

By the time we had five sales centers running across Arizona, New York, New Jersey, and Pennsylvania, I wasn't coaching salespeople anymore. I was coaching the people who coached salespeople. That shift changed the dynamic entirely. When you coach a salesperson, you can watch them, give specific feedback. When you coach a leader, you're getting it secondhand. You have to teach them to see what you would see. To diagnose and fix it themselves.

The first few months, I'd get on calls and tell managers what to do. It worked short term. But two weeks later, a fresh problem would show up. I'd become the bottleneck. Every issue required me.

One afternoon, I was on a call with the Arizona sales manager. He said, "I've got a rep who's closing at thirty percent. Used to be at forty-five. Not sure what changed." Old me would have said, "Okay, here's what you do." And I would have told him exactly how to fix it.

Instead, I said, "What do you think changed?" He paused. "I don't know. That's why I'm calling you." I said, "Have you watched him greet and close lately?" "No. I have been focusing on the new hires."

I said, "Okay. So step one: go watch him. Sit through three closes and take notes. Then call me back and tell me what you saw." He didn't love that answer. He wanted me to tell him what to do.

But I held the line.

Two days later, he called back. "I watched him. He's jumping to payment plans (affordability) glossing over the other boxes. Trying to get to the pricing faster. I think he's anxious about closing, and it's making him skip steps." I said, "Good. So, what are you going to do about it?" He said, "Tell him to slow down?" I said, "Yeah. But more than that. Sit with him. Walk him through why the greet builds like and trust and The Boxes help simplify concerns.

Show him what happens when prospects don't get enough time there. Help him see the pattern, not follow the instruction." He did. The rep's close rate climbed back to forty percent over the next two weeks. That's when I started realizing what my actual job was. I wasn't there to solve problems. I was there to teach leaders how to see problems and solve them themselves. I started changing how I ran coaching calls. Instead of giving answers, I asked questions.

"What do you think is happening?" "What have you tried?" "What did you notice when you watched them?" "If you were in my position, what would you tell you to do?" It felt slower. But over time, the managers stopped needing me as much. They'd see an issue, diagnose it, fix it, and email me after the fact.

Coaching leaders taught me something I didn't expect. The ceiling isn't the system. The ceiling is your ability to develop the people who run the system. If you can't coach leaders, you can't scale. And scaling was the next thing coming.

---

**LESSON IN A BREATH**

*Scaling requires teaching leaders to solve problems, not solving problems for leaders faster.*

---

Scaling requires teaching leaders to solve problems, not solving problems for leaders faster.

## When Systems Break

The call came on a Tuesday afternoon. The Anaheim sales manager. "We've got a problem."

Anaheim was our newest location. Month three. It had started strong.

First week, ten memberships. Second week, thirteen. We were on track.

"What's the problem?" I said.

"Close rate dropped to twenty percent this week. Down from forty. I don't know what happened." That wasn't a slump. That was a system breaking.

I pulled up the dashboard. Appointments were fine. But only six closed.

Out of thirty presentations. The dashboard told me where to look. Without that visibility, I would have been guessing. Something broke down. And I was three thousand miles away.

I got on a call with the sales manager an hour later. "Walk me through what's happening." He said, "I don't know. The team is following the script.

Presentations look fine to me. Prospects aren't buying." I said, "Have you sat through any full presentations this week?" "No. I have been focusing on training the new salesperson.

There it was. He stopped watching. When you stop watching, you stop seeing. And when you stop seeing, problems grow in the dark. I did not know it then, but this was what happens when rhythm fails quietly in the background.

I said, "Okay. Tomorrow, sit through every presentation. Take notes.

Then call me." The next day, he called back. "I think I found it. The pricing section feels off. But I can't figure out what changed." I said, "Send me a recording." Two hours later, I watched the video. He was right. The pricing section was off. But it wasn't what they were saying. It was how they were saying it.

They were apologizing.

Not explicitly. But in their tone. In their body language. "So, um, the membership fee is five thousand dollars. I know that's a lot, but." They were framing the price as something to overcome instead of something worth paying. I watched influence and confidence leak out of their voice long before the prospect said a word.

I'd seen this before. At DirectBuy. At Acura. It happens when a salesperson loses confidence in the product. Or when they internalize too many rejections. They believe the objection before the prospect even says it.

I called the sales manager. "Your team stopped believing in the price.

They're apologizing for it. That's why nobody's buying." He said, "How do I fix that?" I said, "Two things. First, retrain the pricing section. Walk them through the value again. Make sure they can articulate why five thousand dollars is a value for what they're getting. Second, change how you're debriefing after presentations. Stop focusing on what went wrong. Start focusing on what went right. They need to remember what it feels like to close before they can start closing again." He did both. Spent two days retraining. Ran mock presentations where they had to deliver the pricing section with confidence. No apologies.

No hedging. Clear value.

He also changed the team meeting structure. Instead of opening with "What deals did we lose this week?" he opened with, "What went well?" Celebrated the wins. Reinforced what worked.

By the end of the week, the close rate was back to thirty-five percent. Week two, forty percent. Week three, forty-two.

The system didn't break, even though the script changed. It broke because the people executing it stopped believing in it. And belief isn't in the manual. You can't document confidence. Rebuild it.

But here's what bothered me. I caught it because the dashboard showed the drop. The sales manager caught it because I told him what to look for. But what if I hadn't been paying attention? What if the dashboard hadn't flagged it?

The system would have kept breaking. Quietly. Until Anaheim was closing five memberships a week instead of fifteen. And by then, it might have been too late to save.

That's the danger of scaling. Problems don't announce themselves. They show up as small drops in metrics that seem temporary. "Just a bad week." By the time you realize it's not temporary, you've lost a month. Maybe two. I started building early warning systems into the process. Not dashboards. Protocols. It was my first deliberate attempt to bake collapse protection into the way we ran every location.

If any location's close rate dropped more than five points week over week, the sales manager had to send me an email explaining what they saw and what they were doing about it. Not asking permission. Keeping me informed.

If the show rate dropped below forty percent for two consecutive weeks, they had to audit the appointment setters' calls and send me a summary.

If the average sale price dropped, they had to review which tier prospects were choosing and why.

I didn't want to micromanage. But I also couldn't wait for problems to become crises before stepping in. The protocols created a middle ground.

Leaders stayed autonomous, but I stayed aware.

Anaheim taught me something I should have known but didn't fully internalize until it almost cost us a location. Systems don't break loudly. They break quietly. A small crack in confidence. A subtle shift in tone. A script delivered without belief. Years later, that sentence would sit at the heart of collapse prevention.

Systems don't break loudly. They break quietly.

And by the time it shows up in the numbers, it's been happening for weeks.

The best way to prevent that isn't tighter control. It's earlier detection. Building mechanisms that surface problems before they compound. Teaching leaders to see the small cracks before they become fissures.

Because once a system breaks at a distance, fixing it takes ten times longer than preventing it would have.

---

**LESSON IN A BREATH**

*Systems break quietly at a distance; early detection matters more than fast reaction.*

---

Systems break quietly at a distance; early detection matters more than fast reaction.

(A Publicly Traded Higher-Education Corporation, 2021–2025)

I joined a publicly traded higher-education corporation in 2021 and soon after became a senior admissions leader. Multiple campuses nationwide. Over ten areas of study. More than a hundred team members I'd be responsible for leading.

Thousands of students making life-changing decisions about technical education.

It was January 2021. Zoom was standard. Remote work wasn't innovative. It was standard. And higher education was under pressure like never before. Enrollment was down across the industry.

Competition was fierce. And every institution was scrambling to figure out how to operate in a world that had changed.

I was brought in with a clear mandate from leadership: see where the opportunity is. Test your theories. Fix what's broken. But nobody else wanted me there. This was a good old boys' club. An educational establishment where outsiders weren't welcomed. They had refined the admissions process. The compensation was high. The reps were seasoned. The system worked. Or so they thought.

But the numbers told a different story. Conversion rates were stagnant.

The process was bloated. And the leadership culture was profit before people, which meant short-term wins at the expense of long-term trust with students.

The core problem was simple: they pushed "understand before like." They tried to educate students on technical programs before building any relationship. Before earning trust. Before the student even liked talking to them. It was backwards. And it corrupted the entire funnel. It violated the Like → Trust → Understand sequence.

I'd seen this pattern before. At Honda, trust came before value. At Acura, structure protected people. At DirectBuy, I learned that systems scale when you divide labor correctly.

At International Cruise & Excursions, I learned that frameworks have to survive distance.

Here, I had to learn something harder: how to change a system that doesn't want to change. How to prove a better way works when the old way is embedded in culture, compensation, and ego. How to build trust in an environment designed around profit metrics that ignored human behavior.

The opportunity was clear. The resistance was real. And the stakes were higher than anywhere I'd been before. Because this wasn't about sales numbers. It was about students making life-changing decisions. And when you corrupt trust in that context, you don't lose a sale. You lose someone's future.

## The Broken Order

I spent my first two weeks watching. The system was detailed, professional, and thorough. And backwards. They started every conversation with questions about motivation, goals, and income. Technical specifications. Program details. Data before relationship.

It was "understand before like." And it killed trust before trust could even start.

A rep named Tom was on the phone with an 18-year-old potential student about automotive technology.

Tom launched into the curriculum. "Forty-two weeks, thirty hours of class, placement rates, financial aid." More silence.

The kid said, "Okay. Um. Can I think about it, then I'll call you back." And hung up.

Tom put the phone down. Looked frustrated. "He wasn't serious." I said, "Can I ask you something?" He nodded.

I asked, "Did you ask him about where he lived, his interests, his weekend"?

"No" I said, "Did you ask him why he was interested in automotive?" I asked Tom afterward: "Did you ask what he wanted to do with his life?" Tom shrugged. "It's all in the curriculum." I said, "But why? What does he want? What does he care about?" He wouldn't call back. Tom had educated someone who didn't trust him yet.

Same pattern all week. Different reps, different students, same result. Education before connection. The system delivered information but didn't build trust.

By the end of week two, I'd seen enough. I scheduled a meeting with leadership.

"The order is wrong," I said.

They leaned back. "What do you mean?" I told leadership, "We're qualifying and educating before they trust us. Let me pilot something different. One campus. Three months." "The consultants spent two years refining this process. It works." I said, "Then why are conversion rates stagnant?" They didn't have an answer for that. They looked at me for a long moment. Then said, "Which campus?" I said, "Doesn't matter. Pick the one that needs it most." They picked Bloomfield. Decent campus. Average numbers. Nothing special.

Perfect for a test.

At Bloomfield, I explained, "We're changing the order. Connection before education. Why did you reach out? What interests you? What are you hoping for?" Only after they felt heard would we explain the program.

The admissions team didn't look convinced. But they agreed to try.

It felt slow. It felt inefficient. It felt like we were wasting time.

But it worked. Within six weeks, Bloomfield's conversion jumped. Same leads. Same reps. Same market.

Marcus, twelve years in, said: "I've been doing this wrong the whole time. It's not about convincing. It's about helping." They did. Every single time.

**LESSON IN A BREATH**

*Trust comes before teaching; you can't educate someone who doesn't believe you yet.*

Trust comes before teaching; you can't educate someone who doesn't believe you yet.

### Endnotes: The Broken Order

[1] Source Credibility Before Message Content Persuasion effectiveness depends on source credibility and relational trust preceding message content in enrollment and commitment decisions. [2] Pilot Testing in Real Conditions Pilot testing in representative rather than optimal conditions improves external validity and scalability of process interventions. [3] Connection Before Content Relational sequencing in sales processes, prioritizing connection before content delivery, improves conversion across education and service sectors.

## The Contact Center

The Bloomfield pilot proved order mattered. But reps were still doing everything, outbound, inbound, qualifying, presenting, closing. Same problem I'd seen at DirectBuy. One person running an assembly line. I pitched leadership: "Contact center for connection, campus team for closing."

"We tried that five years ago. Students felt handed off." "Because they probably started with the curriculum. Try starting with curiosity."

They said, "Bloomfield again?" I said, "Bloomfield again." We built a contact center team of five. Not salespeople. Contact specialists. Their only job: ask questions and listen.

"What got you interested in automotive?" "What are you hoping to do after you finish?" "Have you worked on cars before?" Let them talk. When they open up, schedule a call with the campus. The first month felt slow. Friction between teams. I told the campus team: "They're handing you warm relationships, not cold leads. Build on it." Within two weeks, friction disappeared. Appointments improved, presentations increased, close rates jumped.

Leadership noticed. Again.

They called me. "How fast can you scale this?" We scaled to thirty specialists across three shifts. Rolled out to all campuses. By year's end, organizational conversions improved substantially.

---

**LESSON IN A BREATH**

*Specialized roles outperform generalists when handoffs protect relationships instead of breaking them.*

---

Specialized roles outperform generalists when handoffs protect relationships instead of breaking them.

## The Zoom Close

Not every student can visit a campus. Some lived hundreds of miles

away. Some were working full-time and couldn't take time off. Some were deciding between programs in different states, and needed to compare options without traveling.

The organization had always struggled with these students. They called them "relocating students" because enrollment meant they'd be moving a distance to attend. High stakes. High commitment. High anxiety.

The old process tried to close them over the phone. It didn't work well. Conversion rates for relocating students lagged far behind local students who could visit campus. That gap was costing hundreds and hundreds of enrollments a year.

The assumption was that you couldn't build the same trust remotely.

That students needed to see the campus, touch the equipment, and meet instructors face-to-face. And while that helped, I didn't think it was the real problem. The real problem was that the phone process still followed the old order. It was transactional. Informational. Reps tried to educate and close without ever building the kind of connection that campus visits naturally create.

By 2021, Zoom wasn't experimental. It was standard. Every student was already comfortable on video calls. The pandemic had normalized it. The question wasn't whether Zoom could work. It was whether we'd use it the right way.

I started testing it with Phoenix relocating students. Instead of phone calls, we scheduled Zoom meetings. Not audio. Video. Face-to-face, even if it was through a screen.

The structure was simple. Contact center qualified interest and scheduled the Zoom call. The campus rep took over from there. Underneath, it was the same divided-lane rhythm I had been building for years.

But instead of launching into the curriculum, they started the same way they would in person. Connection first.

"Tell me what got you interested in diesel mechanics." "What are you hoping this changes for you?" "Have you ever worked on trucks, or is this new?" Let them talk. Build rapport. And then, once there was trust, show them the campus. Virtual tour using screen share. Walk them through the labs.

Show them the equipment. Introduce them to instructors via quick video clips we'd recorded.

It wasn't the same as being there. But it was close enough. And because we'd built the relationship first, and students stayed engaged instead of checking out.

The first month, we tested it with a small group of prospects, and it worked.

That wasn't a fluke. Even through a screen.

We ran it for another month with a larger group, and the conversions held. I took the data to leadership. "Relocating students aren't harder to close. We were using the wrong process. Zoom lets us build the relationship in the same way campus visits do. And when we get the order right, conversion rates match or exceed in-person." They said, "What do you need to scale this?" I said, "Training for every campus team. Equipment for reliable Zoom setups. A library of campus tour videos and instructor introductions so we're not scrambling to show them content in real time." They said, "Do it." We rolled it out over three months. Trained campus reps on how to run Zoom enrollments. Not technically. Behaviorally. How to read body language through a screen. How to build a connection when you can't shake someone's hand. How to close without feeling pushy when you're looking at a camera instead of a person.

Some reps adapted immediately. Others struggled. The ones who relied on physical presence, on walking a student through the shop floor and letting the environment do the selling felt like losing that tool.

I worked with them individually. "The environment helps, but it's not what closes them. What closes them is trust. And you can build trust through a screen, the same way you build it in person. By listening. By caring about them. By making it about their decision, not your enrollment numbers." It took time. But they got there.

By month six, we ran Zoom enrollments across all campuses. Relocating student conversion rates climbed. Hundreds of additional enrollments. All because we stopped treating remote students like second-class prospects and started treating them like people who deserved the same care as anyone who could walk through the door.

Zoom taught me something I'd suspected but hadn't fully proven before.

Proximity doesn't build trust. Presence does. And presence doesn't require you to be in the same room. It requires you to show up fully, pay attention, and make the other person feel like they matter. That insight, especially for leaders and teams who assume influence only works in person.

You can do that through a screen. You can do that across two thousand miles. Get the order right first.

---

**LESSON IN A BREATH**

*Presence builds trust, not proximity; you can show up fully through a screen.*

---

Presence builds trust, not proximity; you can show up fully through a screen.

### Endnotes: The Zoom Close

[1] Video and Social Presence Video-mediated communication enables social presence and relational trust comparable to face-to-face interaction when structured appropriately. [2] Digital Communication Training Systematic training in digital communication behaviors improves remote relationship-building effectiveness beyond technical platform proficiency. [3] Distributed Capability and Continuity Process

resilience through distributed capability development enables organizational continuity during environmental disruptions.

## Resistance

The numbers were undeniable. Contact center adding nine points. Zoom enrollments up eleven. Every pilot worked. But success doesn't eliminate resistance. Sometimes it intensifies it.

Pushback came from three directions: tenured reps who felt threatened, campus directors protecting turf, and executives protecting consultant investments. Greg, a senior Dallas rep, emailed leadership: "I've been enrolling students for fifteen years. My numbers speak for themselves." I didn't respond to the email. I called him.

"Greg, can we talk?" He said, "Sure." I called him. "Your close rate is forty-two percent. The team using the new process is at forty-nine. Seven more students per hundred." He was quiet. "It feels like you're saying I've been doing it wrong." I told him, "You did what you were taught." What you learned was incorrect.

He agreed to try. By week three, his rate had hit 50%.

Campus directors were harder. One, Linda, said: "This doesn't fit our market culture." I said, "The contact center doesn't replace your local relationships. It warms leads before they reach your team." She couldn't argue with the results. Her campus had been flat for two years. Within three months: up ten percent.

Executive resistance was different—not ego, but budget anxiety. Millions invested in consultant systems.

One said, "The old system works. We need better execution." I said, "Then why does every campus that adopts the new order improve?" You can't win everyone over. Some people resist even when the math is irrefutable. You don't need consensus. You need results that speak louder than objections.

Slowly. Painfully. But unmistakably.

---

**LESSON IN A BREATH**

*Resistance doesn't disappear with results; you can't convert everyone, only protect the mission.*

---

Resistance doesn't disappear with results; you can't convert everyone, only protect the mission.

### Endnotes: Resistance

[1] Change Resistance Kotter, J. P. Leading Change, Harvard Business Review Press. Psychological threats to professional identity create resistance to process improvements independent of performance data in tenured employees. [2] Data-Driven Adoption Individual adoption of validated improvements accelerates when personal performance comparisons reveal outcome gaps. [3] Control vs. Outcome Disagreement Middle management resistance in organizational change reflects control concerns rather than outcome disagreements. - Results Over Consensus Universal stakeholder consensus is neither achievable nor necessary for successful organizational change when outcome data validates intervention effectiveness.

## The Framework Emerges

By the second year, I'd stopped thinking about individual

tactics. The order wasn't a sequence anymore. It was a framework.

A way of seeing every interaction, every decision, every system.

It started crystallizing during a training session in Chicago. I was walking a new campus team through the contact center handoff process.

Explaining why the contact center built curiosity instead of delivering curriculum. Why the campus team continued the relationship instead of restarting it. Why education came third, not first. One rep, a younger guy named Jason, stopped me mid-explanation.

"So, they have to like us before they trust us. And they have to trust us before they'll hear what we're teaching them." I paused. That was it. Exactly it. But I'd never said it that cleanly before.

"Yeah," I said. "Like, then trust, then understand. That's the order." He nodded. "And if you skip one, the whole thing breaks?" I said, "Every time." What I'd been building for thirty years wasn't a sales process or an enrollment system. It was a framework for how humans decide. Like comes first. Always. Because if someone doesn't like you, they won't give you the chance to earn trust. And if they don't trust you, they won't believe what you're teaching them.

I started testing it everywhere. Not just enrollment. Leadership meetings. One-on-one coaching. Convincing skeptical directors. The framework worked everywhere because it wasn't about sales. It was about behavior.

I started writing it down. Not for a book. For myself. So I could teach it more clearly.

I showed it to leadership during a quarterly review.

They read it. Looked up. "This is what you've been doing." I said, "This is what's been working." They said, "Can you teach this to everyone?" I said, "I've been trying. But not everyone wants to learn it." They said, "The ones who do are the ones producing results. That's enough." It wasn't enough for me. I wanted everyone to see it. But I was realizing that frameworks don't get adopted because they're right. They get adopted because people see them work and decide they want that outcome for themselves.

By year three, the framework had a name. Not officially. Not in any company document. But the teams that used it started calling it "the order." And when new people joined, they'd ask, "Have you learned the order yet?" It became shorthand. A way of thinking that spread not because I mandated it, but because the people who used it got better results. And results, in the end, are the only argument that matters.

This was the foundation for everything that came after. The framework that would eventually be called ICE. The principles that would apply to industries I hadn't even worked in yet.

The patterns that weren't about enrollment or sales, but about how humans connect, trust, and decide.

It started here. In a training room in Chicago. With a rep named Jason asking the right question. And I finally had the language to answer it.

---

**LESSON IN A BREATH**

*Frameworks emerge when patterns repeat reliably enough to see the universal principle underneath.*

---

Frameworks emerge when patterns repeat reliably enough to see the universal principle underneath.

## The Rollout Complete

Eventually, all campuses ran the same

system. Contact center handling qualification. Campus teams handling relationships and enrollment. Zoom process for relocating students. Like, Trust, Understand protected at every stage.

The numbers told the story. Organizational conversion rate had climbed.

Thousands of additional students enrolled. Not because we worked harder. Because we worked in the right order.

But the rollout wasn't clean. It was messy, political, and exhausting. Every campus had its own resistance. Every director had their own concerns. I spent three years fighting battles I didn't want to fight. Defending a system that should have defended itself with results.

Some campuses adopted enthusiastically. Phoenix, Dallas, Sacramento. Their conversion rates jumped immediately. Others resisted until the data forced compliance. Chicago, Philadelphia, Long Beach. They fought every step until the gap between their numbers and the adopters became indefensible. But not everyone resisted. Two regional directors stood out.

One had quit the company a year before I arrived. Burned out by what he called the "good old boys' club," a culture that rewarded tenure over results and punished anyone who questioned the way things had always been done. When he heard the approach was changing, he came back. Did not need convincing. He had already seen the problem. He just needed someone with the authority to name it.

The other was a woman who had earned deep respect across her region through sheer competence, but who carried real anxiety from years of navigating the old guard. When the new framework rolled out, she did not wait for permission. She installed it immediately, ran it tighter than anyone, and her campus became one of the first to show measurable results.

Neither of them needed the system explained. They needed it protected.

You can't make people care about the right things. You can show them the data. You can prove the system works. But if they care more about protecting their territory than serving the mission, results are the only argument that works.

By year three, the culture had shifted. Not universally.

But enough. New hires learned the framework from day one. Tenured reps who'd adopted it were coaching others. Campus directors were competing to have the best conversion rates, which meant they had to use the system instead of fighting it.

The contact center became the standard. Relocating Zoom enrollments became routine.

The order, like before trust before understand, became the language everyone used even if they didn't all believe in it the same way.

I sat in a leadership meeting in year three when someone said something that surprised me.

"Three years ago, our conversion rate was thirty-seven percent. Kevin told us he could improve it by fixing the order. We didn't believe him.

Some of us still aren't sure we believe him. But the results don't lie. Forty-four percent. That's not luck. That's system design." They looked at me. "I don't know if everyone in this room likes the way we got here. But I know everyone in this room likes the outcome. So whatever resistance is left, it's time to let it go. This is how we work now." It wasn't a ringing endorsement. But it was enough. I went home that night thinking about what the last three years had cost. The fights. The skepticism. The lonely meetings. But it was worth it. Thousands of students enrolled who would have dropped out under the old process. That's not theory. That's real people with real careers.

The rollout was done. The actual work was beginning.

---

**LESSON IN A BREATH**

*Complete rollouts don't require universal belief, undeniable results, and persistent protection of the mission.*

---

Complete rollouts don't require universal belief, undeniable results, and persistent protection of the mission.

Reflections Across Three Decades (1991–2025)

When I stepped into my educational institution chapter, I carried the weight of the largest responsibility of my career. Multiple locations. Across the country. Over a hundred managers and admissions people.

A mission that reached far beyond sales. I was no longer building systems for small teams or helping leaders within a limited environment. I was influencing leaders who were influencing other leaders, all driving results in places I would not see in person.

It forced me to rely not on talent or pressure, but on clarity and rhythm.

As the years unfolded, I saw that everything I had learned over thirty-five years was pointing toward a connected set of principles. Phase six differs from the others. It is not chronological. It is a collection of moments across three decades, where the patterns found their names.

Three moments stand out.

The first was at a poker table in Las Vegas in 2006. That night, under the lights of the World Series of Poker, I learned that trust changes how people play, and that rhythm, when disrupted intentionally, becomes more powerful than skill. 496 entrants, $196,000, and a WSOP bracelet.

No, I have not been back since, but what a memory.

The second was at a conference in New York City. Thousands of people looking for ways to improve their social media presence. A last-second opportunity reminded me that belief and energy can outrun preparation if you are riding the wave.

The third was not a single moment. It was four years of leading at a scale I had never experienced before. From 2021 to 2025, I led over a hundred people across multiple campuses. I was fifty-two when I started.

You cannot lead through control. You cannot lead through proximity. You can only lead through rhythm. And rhythm at scale requires trust in the system more than trust in yourself.

These three moments taught me what I had been building without naming it. And by the end, the framework was complete.

## The WSOP

The World Series of Poker does not care how long you have been playing.

It only cares if you can read the table better than the person sitting across from you.

I have never been a good liar. Not in life, and not at a poker table. In the weekly home games back on Long Island, everyone knew when I tried to bluff. My face would tighten. My voice would change. I eventually stopped trying to bluff the way other people did. I learned to bluff with honesty and ambiguity instead of deception.

If someone said, "You must have a monster hand," I would say, "My cards are pretty good. I wonder if you'll get to find out." If they said, "You missed the draw, right?" I would say, "I'm a terrible artist." All true. All incomplete. Enough to keep me alive in games where everyone else relied on pretending.

That is where I learned you can win by telling the truth in a way that leaves room for interpretation. It worked at the home table, and I carried it with me when I eventually sat at a World Series of Poker table in Las Vegas.

When we reached the final ten players in that tournament, they called a lunch break.

Nine opponents remaining. All of them were stronger technical players than I was. I asked if anyone wanted lunch and offered to pay. Eight accepted. We sat for ninety minutes talking about kids, work, where we lived, and why we played. We talked about everything except poker.

I listened. I asked questions. I treated them like people, not competitors. When we returned to the table, something had changed. The eight who had lunch with me played differently. Their pace shifted. Their bet sizing became more honest.

Their reactions were easier to read. They were not trying to help me. They had simply stopped hiding from me. One by one, they got eliminated.

The one player who did not join us was the last person I faced.

That is how I ended up heads-up with a player who was better than me in every measurable way. It was late in Vegas—the kind of night where the felt starts to blur and the drinks stop tasting like anything. I had been at the table for thirty hours with only a couple of hours of sleep. By a few lucky reads and one good run, I had made it to the final two.

The man across from me looked like he had been carved out of patience. He did not fidget. He did not blink. He did not flinch. He was the kind of player who did not play the cards. He plays the person.

We were nearly even in chips, but I knew the truth. He was better. Technically, statistically, strategically better. If I kept playing at his pace, I would lose slowly.

When they called for a quick break before the last hands, I walked to the bathroom trying to figure out what to do. I understood the situation clearly. I could not outplay him. But I might be able to break his tempo.

So I decided to do something that made no sense on paper.

When we sat back down, I looked him in the eye and chose not to look at my cards.

They call it playing blind. You bet, raise, and call without ever peeking at what you are holding. It sounds reckless, and it is, but I was not trying to win with logic. I was trying to win with rhythm.

The first hand, I raised blind. He hesitated. For a moment, but enough to tell me he was not ready for this.

The second hand, I played blind again. His eyebrows lifted for a second. He was off balance.

Then he went all in. I peeked at my cards and called quickly.

When the cards flipped, the crowd erupted. I had a monster hand.

Two minutes later, it was over.

He was a better player, but I had established my rhythm. For those few hands, rhythm beat skill. That night in Las Vegas gave me an unpolished glimpse of how installing your own cadence creates control.

I did not know the word for it yet, but the lunch was Law 5 before Law 5 had a name. Give first, and the table changes before the cards are dealt.

---

**LESSON IN A BREATH**

*Trust is built in the lunch, not the close; connection beats competence.*

---

Trust is built in the lunch, not the close; connection beats competence.

We booked an event at the Jacob Javits Center. I stood at the booth when one of the conference organizers rushed over. "Hey, we had a speaker cancel. Can you fill in? You go on in twenty minutes." I laughed. "I do not have a presentation." "Talk about what you do. You will be fine." No slides. No notes. No talking points. Me and a microphone.

I walked on stage, introduced myself, and started talking. Why social media matters for realtors. How most of them were doing it wrong. What works. Why authenticity beats gimmick every time.

I figured I would talk for twenty, maybe thirty minutes.

An hour and a half later, I was still going. Not because I was trying to fill time. But because people kept asking questions. And I kept wanting to dig deeper. I had answers. Not because I had rehearsed them. But because I had lived them.

When I finally wrapped up, the room gave me a standing ovation. I walked off stage thinking, "Well, that was weird and fun." Two days later, I got a call.

"Hi, this is Bob from Ms. XX's office. She saw your presentation and wants to talk about bringing your services to her national real estate company." This was one of the most successful real estate moguls in the country. We set up a meeting. Pitched our services.

And we did not get the account.

We were a two-person operation and not able to support a large company with specific needs. The fit wasn't right. But that's not the point.

The point is that when you know your why, it pours out without preparation; opportunities find you. The mogul didn't invite us because we had the slickest presentation. She invited us because she felt our conviction.

**LESSON IN A BREATH**

*Passion without preparation beats preparation without passion every time.*

Passion without preparation beats preparation without passion every time.

## The Patterns Find Their Names

By year three at the higher education company, something had shifted. Not in the results, but in how I saw everything.

I could look at a struggling campus and know exactly where the breakdown was happening. Not because I had been there. But because the patterns were always the same.

Either they were skipping the connection and going straight to education. Or they tried to close before building trust. Or they asked reps to do too much and burn them out. Or they were measuring outcomes instead of behaviors.

Every problem traced back to one of six principles. And once I could see that, I could fix it.

I started writing them down. Not for a book. For myself. So I could teach them more clearly. The raw observations that would eventually become the Six Laws: Skipping connection and jumping straight to education Closing before trust Measuring outcomes instead of behaviors Intensity over rhythm Asking without earning permission first Ignoring the early warning signs of collapse

## Before the Six Laws

You've lived these laws without naming them.

Every time a system collapsed, one of the rules was violated.

Every time they built momentum from nothing, they honored one of them.

Every time a conversation shifted from resistance to possibility, one of them was working beneath the surface.

You felt them in every story you read.

The rhythms that held.

The breakdowns that didn't announce themselves.

The trust that opened doors and the pressure that closed them.

What comes next isn't instruction. It's recognition.

I'm not teaching you six new ideas. I'm giving you names for six patterns you've already experienced. Names that let you diagnose what's breaking before the numbers admit it. Names that let you build systems that don't require you to be the hero.

We start with the failure you fear most, collapse. Then we work backward to the foundation that prevents it.

That's the 6→1 journey.

From the breakdown to the root cause. From the symptom to the system.

From collapse to the single variable that determines if everything else works or fails.

# PART II: THE SIX LAWS

Figure 5: The Rhythm Wave, Six Laws Framework

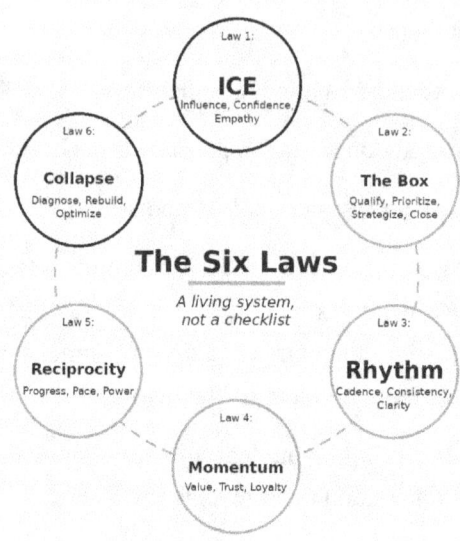

*Figure 5: The Rhythm Wave, Six Laws Framework*

I didn't invent these laws. I gave them a name and a cadence.

Every system I built, across car dealerships, franchise operations, travel companies, and higher education, eventually faced the same test: collapse. Not from a lack of talent. Not from market pressure. From drift. Collapse is predictable. So is preventing it. Rhythm compounds. Urgency exhausts. Maintenance beats rescue. These are not preferences. They are physics.

What follows isn't six disconnected ideas. It's one diagnostic journey.

We start with the breakdown (Law 6: Collapse). The first thing you'll learn is the one thing you must prevent.

Then we build the engine (Laws 5-4-3-2). The system that runs on rhythm, not heroics. That creates movement without pressure. That sustains itself when you're not in the room.

Then we find the root (Law 1: ICE). The one human variable beneath everything. The foundation determines whether it all works or fails.

From collapse to cause. From the failure you fear to the foundation that prevents it. That's how you build rhythm. That's how you protect a system. That's how you lead.

## Why We Begin with Collapse

Most books start with "Step 1." This book doesn't.

Leaders rarely arrive at the beginning of a system. They arrive in Collapse, when dashboards are red, momentum is gone, and trust is thin.

So, we begin where some of you are. Once you understand Collapse, you understand why Momentum matters. Once you understand Momentum, you understand why Rhythm matters. And only then can we move backward to the foundation: The Box and ICE.

To fix the system, we reverse-engineer it. That's why the laws are taught from 6 down to 1.

That is the pattern. Thirty-five years. Five industries. Hundreds of leaders. Thousands of transactions. The same cycle is repeating. The Hero Leader shows up. Carries the team. Fixes the problems. The rhythm breaks the moment they leave. The system collapses without the person.

This is not a style preference. Hero leadership is a structural failure disguised as commitment. It scales until it shatters, and it always shatters.

This book reverses that. It builds systems that run when you are not in the room. Leaders who create rhythms, not rescue missions. Teams that operate with confidence, not dependency.

Part I showed you where these principles came from, the mud, the mistakes, the moments when intuition became system. Part II reveals the architecture beneath those systems. The Six Laws that govern trust, momentum, and sustainable leadership.

You have already seen every law in motion. The shoelace test. The power of silence. The pace you matched without thinking about it. Those were ICE forming before it had a name. The four decisions that stalled every deal you could not close. That was The Box. The Monday meetings and Friday closes that held your strongest months together. Rhythm. The dashboard that showed you what was coming before it arrived. Momentum. The relationships that deepened because you gave before you asked. Reciprocity. The quarter that fell apart after your best month ever. Collapse.

The Six Laws work as a system. But they are not equal.

ICE is the foundation. It is the load-bearing wall. Every other law depends on it, draws from it, or breaks when it erodes. The Box does not work without it. A person will not tell you where their hesitation lives if they do not feel safe enough to be honest. Rhythm does not hold without it. Your team will show up to Monday Reflection and perform instead of reflect if they believe honesty will be used against them. Momentum cannot compound without it. People report real numbers when they trust the system. They report theater when they fear it. Reciprocity does not activate without it. Giving feels genuine when ICE is intact. It feels tactical when it is not. And Collapse always begins with a fracture in ICE. Every breakdown I witnessed across five industries started the same way. Not with a bad quarter. With a relationship that eroded quietly until the system could no longer hold.

You may hear ICE and think it is just another way of saying Like, Trust, and Understand. It is not. Like, Trust, and Understand are experiences. They are what people feel. ICE is the system that governs those experiences and makes them reliable. People can like you without giving you influence. People can trust you without fully understanding you. ICE names the sequence that makes those experiences hold. When the order is right, movement follows. When the order is wrong, everything looks fine until it does not.

That is why the laws are taught from six down to one. We start with the failure you fear and work backward to the foundation that prevents it. By the time you reach ICE, you will understand why it carries the weight of everything above it.

We begin where most leaders are living right now: in collapse.

# Chapter 7: Law 6 – Collapse

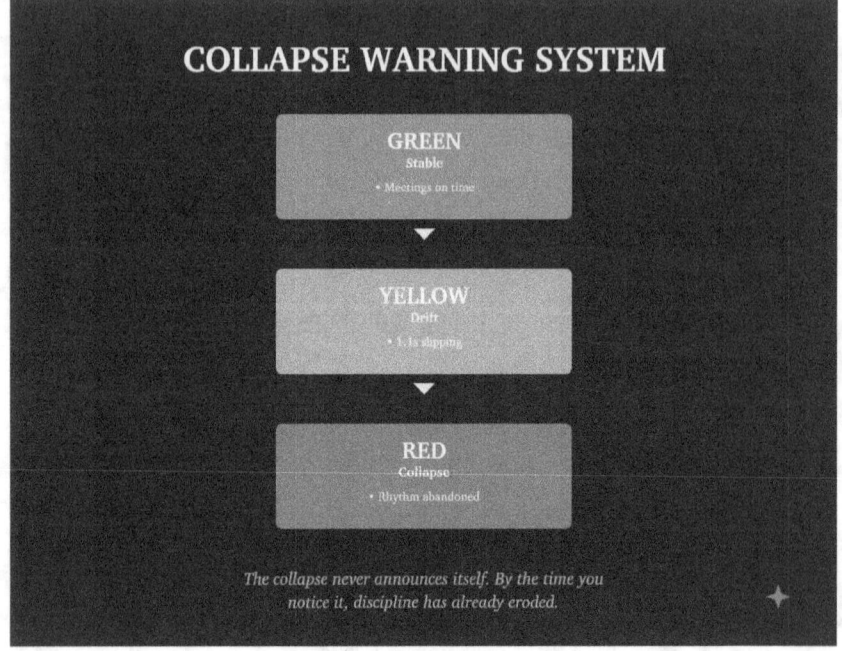

*Collapse Warning System*

Year two at Acura didn't fail because we lacked talent. It failed because discipline softened while success felt stable. That Friday stack I skipped, that Monday meeting I missed. By the time the owner closed his door, the collapse had already happened in the behaviors.

Collapse governs dependence.

Collapse does not start when things fall apart.

It starts when things finally work.

Performance improves. Chaos drops. Systems hold. Leaders feel relief. From the outside, this looks like success.

From the inside, something else begins to form.

Dependence. The earliest version of collapse is subtle. It does not look like failure. It looks like progress that requires supervision.

Decisions move faster when the leader is in the room. Problems resolve cleanly with a single escalation. Alignment sharpens when one person clarifies the thinking.

Results improve.

And quietly, the system begins to lean.

At DirectBuy, the systems worked and performance improved, but leaders relied on me more, not less. When I stepped in, things steadied. When I stepped out, they wobbled. Success didn't remove dependence. It revealed it.

Most leaders misread this moment.

They see improvement and assume the system is working. They see reliance and call it leadership. They accept escalation as proof of trust.

Dependence is not trust.

It is fragility that has not been tested yet.

## The Lifecycle of Collapse

The lifecycle is almost always the same.

Launch. New system, high urgency, simple focus.

Ascend. Early wins, rhythm sets in, belief climbs.

Peak. Habits are strong, results feel easy. This is where danger hides.

Drift. Small compromises, skipped rituals, "this once" becoming "how we do it." Collapse. By the time you see it in the numbers, it has already happened in the behaviors.

The danger is not collapse itself. It is the quiet drift that leads to it. Drift begins at the emotional center. When the pressure of the launch fades, discipline softens. When results feel easy, the process feels optional.[1] That is the trap.

Not a crisis. A comfort.

## The First Collapse

At Acura, by year two, I had built something that worked.

That is when I stopped doing the things that got me there.

A Friday stack skipped here. A Monday check-in missed there. Small compromises. Predictable collapse. For a few weeks, it was fine. The momentum from months of structure carried us. I started thinking maybe I did not need the discipline anymore. Maybe I had outgrown it.

That is the thing about overconfidence. It feels like growth. It feels like you have leveled up. You are ignoring the foundation that is holding everything up.

By the third week, I could feel it. The team grew frustrated. Prospects were less happy. Deals were taking longer to close. The energy that had been effortless was now strained.

The owner came into my office and closed the door. "What's going on? We've been solid for months. Now everything feels chaotic again." He was right. We had lost all discipline. I had stopped doing the work.

Systems do not fail from complexity. They fail from comfort.[2] Remember Anaheim? Conversion rate at 40 percent, team confident, visibility dropped. Within one month: 20 percent. That was collapse in real time. The system breaking quietly while everyone felt secure.

As organizations grow, the cost of dependence rises.

What feels manageable at small scale becomes dangerous at larger scale. The same behaviors that produced results begin to cap them.

Decisions bottleneck. Leaders wait. Momentum slows unless the right person is present.

The system no longer runs on structure.

It runs on availability.

At Acura, my presence raised the level of conversation and clarified decisions, but teams waited for that clarity instead of developing it themselves. Performance held while I was involved. The ceiling appeared when I wasn't. That ceiling is collapse.

Not a drop in numbers.

A limit on independence.

## Listen for Whispers

Collapse never announces itself. It whispers.

Huddles stretch from fifteen minutes to twenty-five. Someone skips practice because it is a busy day. One-on-ones slide from Tuesday to "later this week." Dashboards stop updating because everyone knows how things are going.

Nothing looks broken. The numbers are still fine. That is the danger. Outcomes lag behind behaviors. By the time the metrics admit there is a problem, the habits that matter have been eroding for weeks.

Reps who used to ask for feedback stop asking. Managers who used to prep for meetings start winging them. Leaders who used to be on the floor retreat to their offices. Energy shifts from proactive to reactive.

These are not problems yet. They are signals. If you catch them early, you can correct before collapse. If you miss them, you are rebuilding instead of maintaining.

The early warning signals are specific. Monday Reflections feel rushed or get skipped entirely. Tuesday one-on-ones get rescheduled frequently. Dashboard updates slow down. The team starts celebrating individual wins over system wins. People stop coaching each other and wait for you to intervene.

Watch for the moment when leaders see drift but rationalize it. "We're busy right now." "We'll get back to it next week." That rationalization is the normalization of deviance. Small deviations become accepted over time, eroding the margin until collapse becomes inevitable.

The discipline is not in building the rhythm when things are broken. Anyone can do that. The real discipline is protecting the rhythm when everything seems fine.

One question surfaces drift before it compounds: "Where did the system almost break this week?" Ask it every Monday. The answers will tell you whether the rhythm is holding or slowly unwinding.

## Evolution vs. Drift

Not every change is a collapse. The distinction matters.

Evolution is improvement within structure. Adding a sharper leading indicator to the dashboard. Tightening a coaching question. Adjusting the Wednesday calibration based on what the team has learned. Evolution strengthens the system. Drift is erosion disguised as optimization. Removing Monday Reflection because the team knows what to do. Shortening one-on-ones because everyone seems fine. Letting the dashboard go stale because results are strong. Drift weakens the system while pretending to improve it.

Leaders collapse systems by confusing the two. When success arrives, the instinct to celebrate by loosening structure is predictable and universal. It is also the beginning of collapse. Leaders confuse momentum with immunity. They think they have earned the right to ease off. They have not. They have earned the responsibility to hold tighter.

Collapse is not caused by weak teams.

It is caused by systems that never finish the job.

They improve outcomes but fail to transfer ownership. They stabilize results but centralize judgment. They make leaders effective instead of unnecessary.

That trade feels good at first. Until it breaks.

True mastery does not add control.

It removes it.

A system is not complete when it produces results. It is complete when those results survive the leader's absence.

In higher education, scale forced the issue. Too many campuses and too many leaders made constant intervention impossible. Stability without me stopped being a goal and became a requirement.

Collapse was designed out by design.

## Optimizing for Removal

When Collapse is addressed correctly, leaders stop optimizing for visibility and start optimizing for removal.

They build systems that answer questions without escalation. They create rhythms that surface issues early. They install clarity that does not require interpretation.

Performance no longer depends on presence.

It depends on structure.

You know the system is working when Monday Reflection begins without prompting. When the team uses Box language naturally. When dashboard updates are automatic. When people coach each other without needing you. When drift is named and corrected within a day.

Those are not aspirational goals. They are the minimum standard for a system that survives its builder.

The goal is stability without stagnation. Discipline without pressure. A team operating on rhythm, not adrenaline. This is why Collapse comes first.

Understanding collapse is why the other five laws exist. Every law you read in this book exists because I watched what happens when it is missing. Reciprocity breaks down when you ask before you give. Momentum stalls when you chase outcomes instead of behaviors. Rhythm dies when discipline softens. The Box fails when you stop diagnosing. And underneath all of it, ICE determines whether any of it holds.

If dependence is not addressed, every other Law eventually feeds it. Rhythm becomes routine without ownership. Influence becomes persuasion without transfer. Structure becomes compliance without judgment.

Everything works.

Until it doesn't. Collapse is not a warning.

It is a diagnostic.

If performance drops when the leader steps away, the system was never finished.

If you remember one thing from this Law, remember this.

Success that requires you is temporary.

Stability that survives you is the goal.

Collapse governs whether you are building a system or becoming the system.

It is a law.

**LESSON IN A BREATH**

*Collapse whispers before it screams. Protect the behaviors that created the win long after the win arrives.*

Collapse whispers before it screams. Protect the behaviors that created the win long after the win arrives.

### Endnotes: Collapse

[1] Leading Indicators and Early Warning Behavioral metrics predict performance changes weeks before outcome metrics reflect them. By the time results decline visibly, process failures have already compounded. [2] Normalization of Deviance Vaughan, D. The Challenger Launch Decision: Risky Technology, Culture, and Deviance at NASA. System failures rarely result from dramatic breakdowns. Small deviations become accepted over time, eroding safety margins until collapse becomes inevitable.

# Chapter 8: Law 5 – Reciprocity

## Law 5: Reciprocity

*Give, Receive, Commit*

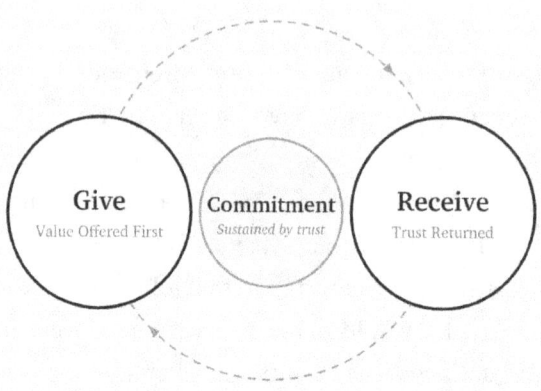

*Law 5: Reciprocity – Give, Receive, Commit*

At International Cruise and Excursions, shoppers were avoiding us like we were handing out subpoenas. We were asking before we gave. The moment we reversed that order, everything changed. That reversal is this Law.

That avoidance was not a marketing failure. It was a violation of human equilibrium. That reversal revealed a Law. Reciprocity governs ownership transfer.

Most leaders think reciprocity is about being fair or being liked.

It isn't.

Reciprocity determines whether responsibility moves back across the line or stays parked with the leader. When it works, ownership spreads. When it breaks, leaders carry more than they should, even when systems look sound. Reciprocity answers one simple question.

Who is actually holding the work?

Most sales teams fail this sequence: they ask before they give. They pitch before they listen. They close before they connect. The order is wrong, and it kills the relationship before it starts.

You cannot ask before you give. And you cannot give with an agenda and expect it to work. Reciprocity is the Law that converts service into permission, permission into curiosity, and curiosity into movement.

At International Cruise and Excursions, we learned that giveaways create activity, not ownership. We could smooth the handoff and keep leads moving, but until commitment was built through real conversations, the work never truly crossed the line.

That experience is where this Law comes from.

## Why Reciprocity Works

That avoidance we saw at the kiosks was not bad luck. It was a violation of human equilibrium. Human behavior is governed by an internal sense of balance. When someone gives us something meaningful without expectation, a natural tension forms. We feel a subtle pull to close the loop. This is not guilt. It is equilibrium.

Psychology calls this the norm of reciprocity, a mechanism that maintains cooperation inside groups.[1] Leaders experience this everywhere.

You give someone your time; they give you their trust.

You offer clarity; they offer truth.

You invest in their success; they invest in the system. People rarely say, "I feel obligated because you helped me." They simply behave differently. They lean in. They stop protecting themselves. They start contributing. Think about the poker lunch. Nobody asked anyone to show up differently. The environment changed, and behavior followed.

Reciprocity lowers defensiveness and raises openness. It shifts the brain from scanning for threat to scanning for possibility.[2] Helping without expectation triggers emotional openness. Pressure collapses it instantly.

Most salespeople misunderstand this Law. They think reciprocity is about giving trinkets, offering bonuses, or adding a gimmick to an ask. But reciprocity only activates when the other person feels genuinely helped, not strategically nudged. The gift that activates reciprocity is never a pen or a coffee. It is attention, clarity, or space. Reciprocity is not a tactic. It is a shift in state. A human response to feeling seen, supported, and safe.

When reciprocity is working, the prospect moves toward you voluntarily. When it is missing, every interaction feels like pressure.

## The Field Lesson

At DirectBuy, I watched this principle work in real time. A prospect would call, frustrated by pricing and overwhelmed by the process. The customer service representative could have launched into a defensive pitch immediately. Most companies do.

Instead, the rep spent five minutes listening. Validated the frustration. Explained how the membership worked without defending the small margins on electronics. Offered to send a simple breakdown of how much they could save on their specific project with no appointment required.

The prospect seemed surprised. They gave their email and walked away.

That email was pure reciprocity. No strings. No pressure. Value first.

Three days later, the prospect called back and scheduled the appointment themselves. They felt safe enough to move forward because we had given before we asked. Reciprocity had converted curiosity into permission.

The reps who understood this principle closed at noticeably higher rates than those who treated the first call like a battle to win.

At International Cruise and Excursions, the team learned that you cannot ask for engagement until you have created value first. Not theoretical value. Actual value the shopper can feel. When the team began helping without an agenda, everything changed. Eye contact returned. Conversations lengthened. Even store employees began directing people to the kiosk.

The principle is the point: Serve first. Then ask. Not the other way around.

## How Reciprocity Fails

Reciprocity rarely fails loudly.

It fails quietly, through help. Leaders step in to remove friction. They smooth handoffs. They solve objections early. They protect momentum. Results look good. Conversion holds. Activity stays high.

And ownership never forms.

What feels like support slowly becomes substitution.

When reciprocity is missing, effort flows in one direction.

Leaders give clarity.

Leaders give energy.

Leaders give protection.

Teams receive direction, but they do not carry responsibility. Accountability turns into compliance. Progress depends on reminders instead of commitment. That imbalance is exhausting.

And easy to miss.

Reciprocity breaks down in predictable ways.

Giving with pressure baked in. "Let me help you so you'll owe me." People feel the hook instantly. The gift becomes a transaction, and trust collapses before it forms.

Giving something trivial and expecting something meaningful back. A free pen does not earn life-changing decisions. The size of the gift must match the weight of the ask.

Asking too early. Asking before anything has been given triggers defensive psychology. The brain shifts from openness to protection, and once that shift happens, it is difficult to reverse.[3] Confusing friendliness with contribution. Being nice is not the same as creating value. People appreciate warmth. They reciprocate substance.

Reciprocity cannot be faked. People feel intent the way animals sense danger.

At Acura, when I stopped filling silence and let the room work, something changed. People corrected me. They pushed back. Responsibility came back across the table without being demanded.

Reciprocity didn't improve because trust was discussed.

It improved because space was created for return.

## The Leader's Application

Reciprocity is not only a consumer dynamic. It is a leadership dynamic.

Teams reciprocate what they consistently receive.

If leaders give clarity, teams give truth. If leaders give presence, teams give effort. If leaders give calmness, teams give confidence. If leaders give development, teams give commitment. But if leaders give chaos, teams return chaos. If leaders give pressure, teams return avoidance.

Everyone wants loyalty. But loyalty is reciprocity in disguise. It is not earned through authority. It is earned through service. Leaders earn commitment the same way salespeople earn trust. Not by asking for it. By creating the conditions where it forms on its own.

## Reciprocity in Practice

Reciprocity is not something you install once. It lives in the daily interactions between leader and team, between team and customer.

The practical test is simple. In every interaction, ask whether value was given before commitment was requested. Send a resource before the follow-up call. Offer clarity before asking for a decision. Solve a minor problem before presenting the big solution. When prospects and team members feel helped before they are asked, reciprocity activates naturally. The ask feels like the next step in a relationship, not an interruption.

The most common failure mode is fake reciprocity. Teams confuse tactics with service. "I'll give you this free thing if you schedule a call." Prospects feel the hook instantly. Give without strings. Ask without pressure. Trust the sequence.

When prospects say "I need to think about it" and then disappear, reciprocity has already failed. Either the hesitation was never diagnosed, or value was never given first. That is not a closing problem. That is a sequence problem. The Box tells you where the hesitation lives. Reciprocity tells you whether you earned the right to address it.

Reciprocity does not come from motivation.

It comes from structure.

When systems do too much for people, they quietly train dependence. When systems require contribution, ownership begins to move.

This is why good intentions often make things worse.

Helping too early removes the need to engage. Protecting too much removes the need to prepare. Explaining everything removes the need to think.

The work stays with the leader.

## What Reciprocity Requires

Reciprocity requires three commitments.

First, give something real before asking for anything. Not information. Not clever phrasing. Something useful. Second, ask naturally, not forcefully. The ask should feel like the next step in a relationship, not a transaction.

Third, maintain the balance. If people feel you are taking more than you give, reciprocity collapses.

## The Sequence That Makes Reciprocity Work

Reciprocity cannot stand alone. It requires Momentum to create opportunities worth serving. Rhythm to make service consistent. ICE to ensure service feels safe rather than strategic.

Reciprocity is the emotional engine. Momentum creates the activity flow. Rhythm creates the cadence. ICE creates the trust. Together they form the foundation for influence.

When any of these laws weaken, reciprocity suffers. Without Momentum, there are not enough interactions to build the pattern. Without Rhythm, service becomes sporadic instead of reliable. Without ICE, generosity feels strategic instead of genuine. Reciprocity holds when the system underneath it holds.

Reciprocity is often confused with compliance.

Compliance looks like agreement.

Reciprocity looks like contribution.

Compliance follows direction.

Reciprocity carries load.

You can have a disciplined team with very little reciprocity. You cannot have a resilient system without it.

In higher education, scale forced reciprocity to be designed. Leaders were expected to think, challenge, and carry weight. Ownership became mutual because it had to.

That shift changed everything.

The leader stopped being the emotional buffer. The system started carrying itself.

This is why Reciprocity follows Collapse.

Collapse reveals dependence. Reciprocity determines whether that dependence ever reverses.

Without reciprocity, rhythm becomes routine. Influence becomes persuasion. Structure becomes enforcement.

Everything looks organized.

Nothing scales.

If you remember one thing from this Law, remember this.

Giveaways create activity.

Relationships create ownership. Reciprocity governs whether the work actually crosses the line.

It is a law.

**LESSON IN A BREATH**

*Give before you ask. Serve before you sell. The door opens when they open it.*

Give before you ask. Serve before you sell. The door opens when they open it.

### Endnotes: Reciprocity

[1] Gouldner, A. W. "The Norm of Reciprocity," American Sociological Review. The norm of reciprocity operates as a fundamental mechanism maintaining cooperation within groups through balanced exchange. [2] Cialdini, R. "Reciprocity Rule," Influence: The Psychology of Persuasion. When people receive genuine help without expectation, their defensive responses decrease and they become more open to possibilities. [3] Premature Ask Response Premature requests activate threat detection in the amygdala, pushing people into protective states that block openness and forward movement.

# Chapter 9: Law 4 – Momentum

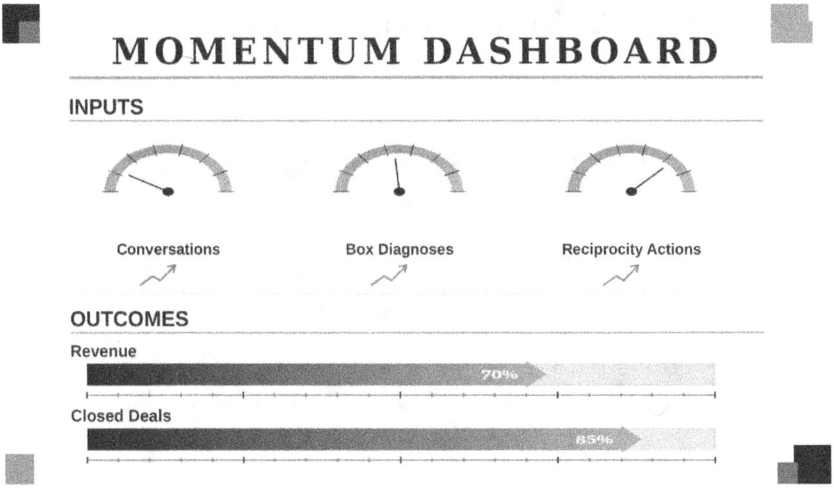

## MOMENTUM DASHBOARD

INPUTS

| Conversations | Box Diagnoses | Reciprocity Actions |
|:---:|:---:|:---:|

OUTCOMES

Revenue

70%

Closed Deals

85%

*Figure 8: Momentum Dashboard*

The $150 prospect wasn't about math. It was about carryover. Every person who walked onto that Honda lot carried the same value regardless of whether they bought. That was the first time effort had somewhere to land instead of resetting every morning.

Momentum governs whether effort compounds or resets.

Most teams confuse momentum with activity.

Phones are ringing. Calendars are full. People are working hard. It looks like progress. It feels exhausting.

The problem is not motion.

The problem is that nothing carries.

At Honda, the commissions mindset kept resetting progress. If a deal didn't close, the day felt wasted. Effort only counted when it paid. The $150 customer changed that. Even without a sale, work carried forward, and momentum finally had something to build on. That moment is where this Law begins.

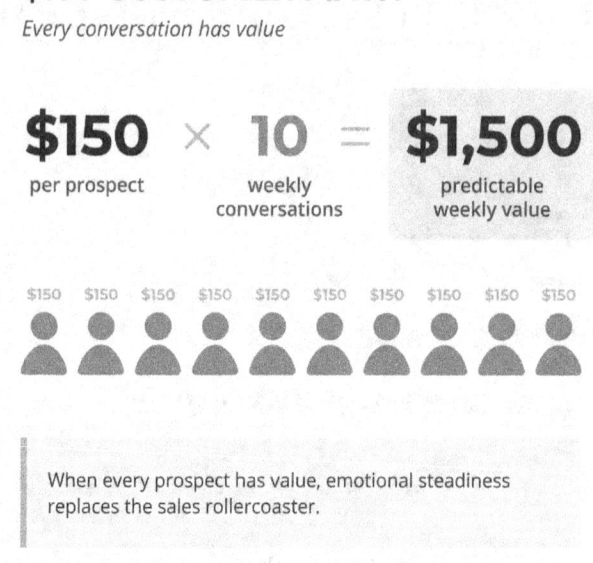

Figure 7: $150 Customer Math – Every Conversation Has Value

Momentum does not come from intensity.

It comes from carryover.

When effort only matters if it closes today, every day becomes a reset. Wins spike emotion. Losses erase progress. Teams stay busy, but nothing compounds. That is what a commissions mindset does.

It rewards motion and punishes continuity.

Momentum appears the moment effort has a place to land.

When something small carries forward regardless of outcome, the system starts stacking progress. Energy stabilizes. Focus sharpens. People stop feeling like yesterday disappeared.

Momentum does not require big wins.

It requires continuity.

This is why so many teams feel stuck even while moving fast.

They are running systems that erase yesterday.

Activity replaces accumulation. Urgency replaces direction. Effort resets instead of stacking. It looks like hustle.

From the inside, it feels like starting over.

At Acura, momentum showed up again when the same questions were allowed to carry from one meeting to the next instead of being replaced by urgency. Decisions started lasting because thinking stopped resetting.

Nothing sped up.

Things finally stuck.

Momentum is not created by doing more.

It is created by doing something that carries.

When conversations continue instead of restarting, decisions gain weight. When learning returns instead of floating, progress compounds.

This is also why momentum disappears under pressure.

Urgency demands action now. Carryover feels slow. Leaders step in. Problems get solved. The next moment arrives with no memory of the last one.

The system moves.

Progress does not.

In higher education, momentum had to be designed. Cadence created carryover across weeks and terms, so progress accumulated without constant pressure.

That shift changed how momentum worked.

Momentum stopped being emotional.

It became structural.

## The $150 Prospect

At Honda, one simple calculation changed the way I saw the entire job. Five sales out of ten prospects. Average commission of three hundred dollars. Ten prospects per week meant fifteen hundred dollars earned. Divide that by ten prospects, and every human being who walked through the door was worth one hundred fifty dollars.

It did not matter when they arrived. It did not matter if they were serious. It did not matter whether they bought today or next year. The value was the same.

This simple arithmetic removed the emotional rollercoaster. I stopped celebrating too intensely after wins. I stopped collapsing after losses. I focused on conversations, not closes. When the number of meaningful conversations stayed consistent, the sales stayed consistent too.

Momentum is emotional neutrality combined with behavioral discipline.[1]

## Why Visibility Beats Motivation

Motivation depends on energy, mood, weather, external pressure, incentives, and the unpredictable emotional cycles of human beings. Visibility does not. Visibility turns uncertainty into direction.

Once I could see exactly where deals were stalling, I no longer had to guess. When I could see which behaviors predicted progress, I no longer hoped. Motivation spikes briefly. Visibility compounds steadily.[2] You cannot fix what you cannot see.

You cannot see what you do not track.

You cannot track what you have not defined.

Momentum is the accumulation of clear definitions.

By the time I was leading more than a hundred admissions representatives across multiple campuses, I had learned this the hard way. When numbers slipped, people reached for opinions rather than data. "I think it is the leads." "I think it is the reps." "I think it is the economy." Opinion is a terrible operating system. It creates the illusion of insight without the precision of diagnosis. When leaders rely on opinion, they either pressure the team or blame the team. Both responses produce short bursts of activity followed by collapse.

Momentum requires something different. It requires a system that shows what is happening, not what you feel is happening. That is the discipline of visibility.

## Building the Dashboard

We started with backward design. What cost per enrollment can we sustain as a business model? From there, we built upstream. Enrollments. Appointments. Contacts. Leads. Behaviors. Which behaviors at each stage predict the next one? Which are noise? Which are signals? What needs coaching? The purpose of dashboards is not to obsess over numbers. They exist to create diagnostic conversations. A leader cannot coach a mystery. A mystery forces you into motivational speeches. Motivation can sometimes worsen the problem by accelerating the wrong behaviors. Diagnosis fixes the problem by aligning behavior with outcomes.

If the speed-to-lead was slow, we fixed it. If confirmation calls were sloppy, we scripted the mirror-back and practiced it until it was clean. If trust did not transfer in the handoff, we listened to the calls together. Momentum is not about working harder. It is about working on the right thing. Visibility tells you which thing is the right thing.

Over time, that discipline produced real growth. Not through intensity. Through consistency rooted in clarity. Momentum is predictable when visibility is strong.

The dashboard tracks inputs, not outcomes. New conversations initiated. Follow-ups completed. Pipeline additions. Box-based diagnoses. Those are the numbers that tell you what is actually happening. Closes, revenue, and conversion rates are lagging indicators. They tell you what already happened. Leading indicators tell you what is about to happen. Start with three to five inputs. Add more only after the first set becomes automatic. Leaders who build dashboards with fifteen metrics end up with teams that ignore all of them.

When the dashboard is visible and the team reviews it at the start of each week, conversations shift. People stop saying "I had a bad week" and start saying "I only had two conversations." That is the shift. That is momentum becoming structural. The team starts diagnosing their own performance gaps instead of waiting for someone to tell them what went wrong.

## The Momentum Curve

Most teams imagine momentum as acceleration. In reality, momentum is continuity. It is a smooth transfer of energy across the entire decision arc. The behavior at the top of the funnel creates the pace at the bottom. Small bottlenecks upstream create major losses downstream.

Momentum follows a predictable curve: Behavior produces consistency of behavior. Consistency produces pattern recognition. Pattern recognition produces coaching alignment. Coaching alignment produces predictable outcomes.

Teams that collapse never collapse at the outcome stage. They collapse at stages one and two. Behavior is inconsistent. They try new things every week. They treat fluctuations as mysteries instead of signals. They chase results instead of generating momentum.

Leaders who master Momentum stay upstream. They coach the stage where change is cheap and impact is high. When someone complains about results, the question is not "What happened?" The question is "What inputs were missing?" Every time. Even when it is uncomfortable. Coaching the close feels more decisive. Coaching the conversation is what actually works.

## What Momentum Requires

Momentum needs four elements, all measurable, all coachable.

Leading Indicators. These are the behaviors that precede success. Conversations, contacts, confirmations, follow-ups, cadence checks. Leading indicators give you early warnings and early wins.

Emotional Neutrality. Teams fall apart when they ride the highs and lows of weekly results. Emotional neutrality allows them to stay consistent long enough for the system to work. Leaders set the tone. Calm is contagious.

Upstream Correction. Leaders lose Momentum when they wait too long to intervene. Upstream correction is surgical. You adjust the smallest controllable behavior that influences the larger outcome.

Cadence. Momentum collapses without rhythm. Rhythm allows you to sustain momentum without burning out. Law 3 and Law 4 operate as a pair. Rhythm stabilizes the environment. Momentum directs the behavior.

# Why Leaders Misdiagnose Momentum Problems

Most momentum breakdowns masquerade as talent problems. Someone underperforms. The leader questions commitment. They question skill. They question motivation.

But when you look at the dashboard, the truth is simpler. They made fewer contacts. They missed Tuesday coaching. They drifted off rhythm. They let emotional volatility disrupt visibility.

Momentum problems are rarely character problems. They are pattern problems.

One of the most common misdiagnoses is the team that is closing deals while the pipeline empties. Results look strong. Everyone relaxes. But the inputs have vanished while the outcomes distracted attention. By the time the pipeline catches up to the truth, the team is two weeks behind and scrambling. The dashboard would have caught it. The dashboard always catches it.

Momentum generates the wins that make Reciprocity possible. But momentum must live inside a consistent cadence, or it turns into spurts. Without Rhythm, Momentum becomes erratic. Without Momentum, Rhythm becomes hollow. These laws reinforce each other.

When Momentum is strong, results feel fair. When Momentum is weak, results feel arbitrary. When results feel arbitrary, people stop believing in the system. When they stop believing, Collapse begins.

Momentum protects the team from the emotional fog that leads to Collapse. That is why it is one of the Six Laws.

Momentum stabilizes teams in a way speed never can.

When effort compounds, people stop chasing results. They start trusting the process. Progress feels calmer even as it accelerates.

That calm is not comfort.

It is traction. This is why Momentum sits where it does.

Without Momentum, Rhythm becomes maintenance. Reciprocity becomes transactional. Collapse becomes inevitable.

Systems that do not compound will always feel heavier over time.

If you remember one thing from this Law, remember this.

Motion feels productive.

Carryover is productive.

Momentum governs whether yesterday matters today. It is a law.

---

**LESSON IN A BREATH**

*Momentum lives in the behaviors you repeat, not in the results you hope for.*

---

Momentum lives in the behaviors you repeat, not in the results you hope for.

### Endnotes: Momentum

[1] Emotional Neutrality and Decision Quality Emotional neutrality improves decision-making under pressure by reducing cognitive overload and anchoring attention on controllable inputs rather than uncontrollable outcomes. [2] Visibility Over Motivation Systematic visibility into leading indicators produces more reliable performance improvements than extrinsic motivation alone. Visibility creates self-correction loops. Motivation does not.

# Chapter 10: Law 3 – Rhythm

## Law 3: Rhythm

*Cadence, Consistency, Clarity*

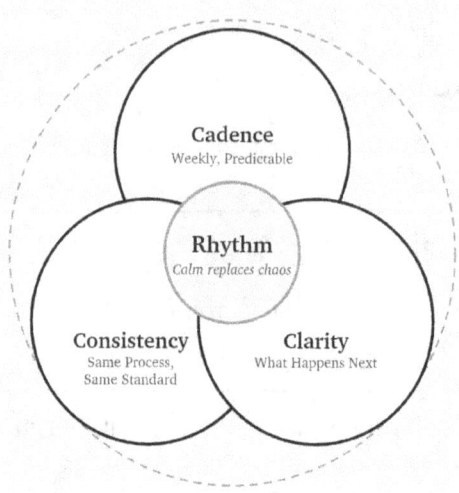

**Cadence**
Weekly, Predictable

**Rhythm**
*Calm replaces chaos*

**Consistency**
Same Process,
Same Standard

**Clarity**
What Happens Next

*Law 3: Rhythm – Cadence, Consistency, Clarity*

At Honda, every week felt like a fresh start. Nothing stacked. At Acura, the same issues kept recurring until we went back to what happened last time before moving forward. That return is where Rhythm lives.

Rhythm governs performance stability.

If you have ever led a team that felt capable but unpredictable, you already know what this Law is about.

Most leaders explain inconsistency as a people problem. Focus drifts. Accountability slips. Energy rises and falls. When results swing, the instinct is to apply pressure. More meetings. More urgency. More involvement. That response feels responsible.

It is also aimed at the wrong thing.

What breaks first is rarely commitment.

What breaks is cadence.

Rhythm governs whether performance stabilizes or swings as conditions change. When rhythm holds, results settle. When rhythm breaks, outcomes fluctuate, even with good people doing their best.

At Honda, every week felt like a fresh start. Deals got done, problems got handled, and then the next week arrived with nothing carrying over. Effort stayed high, but nothing ever stacked.

Instability rarely shows up as failure.

It shows up as variance.

A strong stretch followed by a scattered one. Momentum that feels real until it suddenly isn't. Leaders call this inconsistency, but inconsistency is only the symptom.

The cause is that learning never returns to the same place.

When reflection happens randomly, teams solve problems in the moment. Reaction replaces pattern recognition. Over time, even strong people start to feel unreliable in systems that never return to the same conversation twice.

That is not a people problem.

It is structural.

Rhythm is often mistaken for consistency.

Leaders hear the word and think routine. Doing the same things on the same days. When that breaks down, they assume the system failed. That's backward.

Consistency is not the cause.

Consistency is the result.

Rhythm is the system that decides whether learning returns or drifts.

At Acura, leadership meetings kept reopening the same issues until the conversation slowed and we started coming back to what happened last time before moving on. That's when things finally began to settle.

As results continued to swing, another pattern emerged.

The fastest way to steady things was to step in. Clarify decisions. Remove friction. Make calls. The team felt relief. Performance improved.

Briefly. Then it happened again.

Later, as the teams got bigger, every time I stepped in to steady results, performance improved in the moment but leaned more on me and less on the system. That's when it became clear that stability was being borrowed, not built.

When the leader becomes the stabilizer, the system stops carrying weight.

Decisions bottleneck. Learning thins out. Conversations repeat. Momentum depends on presence instead of process.

It looks like leadership.

It feels like progress.

It is neither.

It is load-bearing.

## What Rhythm Means

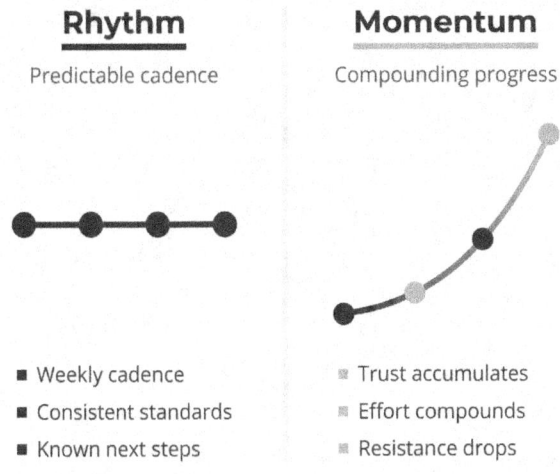

# Rhythm vs Momentum
## Stability vs Acceleration

| Rhythm | Momentum |
|---|---|
| Predictable cadence | Compounding progress |

- Weekly cadence
- Consistent standards
- Known next steps

- Trust accumulates
- Effort compounds
- Resistance drops

*Figure 9: Rhythm vs Momentum, Stability vs Acceleration*

Rhythm is the predictable sequence of behaviors that stabilizes performance. It is not motivational. It is mechanical. When people know what happens on Monday, Tuesday, Wednesday, Thursday, and Friday, they stop spending emotional energy trying to decode the workflow and start spending it on the work. Most teams confuse busy with rhythmic. Busy is chaotic. Rhythmic is intentional.

Rhythm answers five questions without anyone needing to ask them: What are we focused on today? How do we know we are on pace? How do we adjust in real time? How do we end the week clean? How do we prepare for next week?

When leaders answer those questions in a structured way, they stop reacting and start diagnosing.

A chaotic system makes every problem feel urgent.

A rhythmic system makes every problem feel solvable.

## The Five-Day Flow

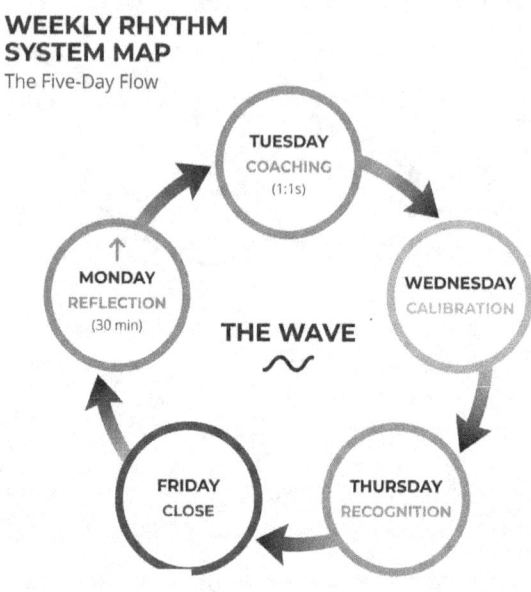

*Figure 12: Weekly Rhythm System Map – The Five-Day Flow*

The breakthrough came when I stopped asking who was working hardest and started defining what a good week looked like. Rhythm is the architecture of a good week.

Monday: Reflection.

The week starts with clarity. What worked, what did not, and why. Not an emotional download, but a structural one. Reflection sharpens pattern recognition. Top performers reflect instinctively. Teams need a process for it. On Mondays, the goal is not motivation. It is alignment. You cannot coach forward if you do not understand backward. When Monday becomes a day for reporting numbers instead of learning, the week loses its rhythm before it starts. The team performs instead of thinking. They tell you what you want to hear instead of what they actually learned. The fix is not to push harder. The fix is to ask, "What did you learn?" instead of "What did you close?" Tuesday: Coaching. Coaching is not a list of everything someone could improve. It is one behavior, clearly defined, with a measurable way to practice it. Fifteen minutes is enough when the behavior is specific. Too many leaders confuse coaching with correcting. Correction fixes mistakes. Coaching builds capability. The one-on-one is where rhythm either strengthens or erodes. The goal is not to solve their problems. The goal is to help them solve their own problems while feeling supported. When someone surfaces a challenge, the instinct is to fix it. That builds dependency. The better move is to stay in the question long enough for them to find their own answer.

Wednesday: Calibration.

Midweek is where drift becomes visible. Drift is subtle at first. Slight misses. Small inconsistencies. A call not logged. Someone skipped a follow-up. Drift multiplies if uncorrected. Calibration is not a meeting. It is a pulse check. Are we on pace? Are we behind? Which behaviors need tightening? When something is off track, the question is not "What happened?" The question is "Where in the Box does the hesitation live?" That reframes friction as information rather than failure. Once the team can name the hesitation, they can solve it. Diagnose on Wednesday. Drill on Thursday. Do not try to fix both in the same conversation.[1] Thursday: Celebration.

Most teams celebrate outcomes. Rhythmic teams celebrate behavior. Recognition reinforces what you want repeated. The team hears what the culture values. If you celebrate results alone, you end up glorifying heroics. If you celebrate rhythm, you reinforce the system.

Friday: Preparation.

The week closes clean. No open loops. No loose ends. No unresolved commitments drifting into Monday. A clean Friday produces a calm Monday. The Friday close is not a celebration and not a postmortem. It is a reflection that turns the week's experience into next week's intelligence. Run it even when the week went well. Especially when the week went well. When leaders skip it during good weeks, drift begins. Success creates the illusion that structure is optional.

Installing the Flow Do not install all five days at once. That is how rhythm becomes another burden instead of a relief.

Start with Monday. Just the reflection. Run it for two weeks until it feels normal, not forced. Then add Tuesday coaching. One behavior per person. Fifteen minutes. Nothing more. Once Monday and Tuesday hold, Wednesday calibration will feel like the natural next question: are we on pace?

Most teams can install the full Five-Day Flow in four to six weeks. The teams that try to launch everything on a Monday morning usually abandon it by Wednesday. Rhythm is built the same way trust is built. Gradually. Consistently. Without force.

When I installed the Five-Day Flow across fifteen campuses, we did not mandate it simultaneously. We started with three campuses. Let the pattern settle. Let the early adopters report what was working. Then the remaining campuses asked to join because they saw the results, not because they were told to comply. That is rhythm selling itself.

## Why Rhythm Works

Rhythm works because it creates return.

Not return to a plan.

Return to a conversation. When teams know there is a place where learning will be addressed before urgency takes over, problems stop

140

stacking. Reflection becomes expected instead of optional.

That is when performance begins to stabilize.

Not because people try harder.

Because the system stops letting things drift.

When show rates dropped one quarter, everyone wanted a pep talk. But pep talks do not repair drift. Cadence repairs drift. We traced the breakdown and found it quickly. Monday reflections had loosened. Tuesday one-on-ones had slipped into casual check-ins. Wednesday reviews had shifted toward outcomes instead of behaviors. The system had drifted. Rhythm had broken. Once we reinstalled the cadence, performance recovered. Not through emotion. Through structure.[2] Rhythm is not glamorous. Rhythm is not dramatic. That is why it works. It protects performance from your mood.

## Protecting Rhythm

Most rhythm breakdowns do not come from neglect.

They come from good intentions.

A busy week pushes reflection aside. A quick fix replaces return. Urgency gets rewarded just often enough to weaken the pattern.

Each interruption sends the same message.

Speed matters more than return.

Over time, instability creeps back in.

Protecting rhythm requires restraint.

It means resisting the urge to solve too early. Allowing conversations to slow before speeding up. Trusting that coming back is more powerful than reacting.

This is hardest for capable leaders.

High performers are wired to act. Rhythm asks them to pause.

That pause is not inaction.

It is structure.

The fastest diagnostic for drift is the calendar. Did Monday Reflection happen every week at the same time? Did Tuesday one-on-ones happen for every person? Did the Wednesday check happen without skipping? Did Friday Close happen even when the week went well? If the answer to any of those is no, drift has already begun. You do not need a complicated audit. You need to look at whether the cadence held. Protect the rhythm most when you feel like you need it least.[3]

## Why Heroes Fail

Heroic leaders create dependence. Rhythmic leaders create capability.

The organization that celebrates its hero is celebrating its single point of failure.

The Hero Leader solves everything personally. The Rhythm Leader builds a system that solves predictably. Hero-led organizations are reactive. Rhythmic organizations are proactive. Hero-led cultures follow charisma. Rhythmic cultures follow structure. Heroics collapse under scale. Rhythm scales naturally.

Hero leaders win moments. Rhythmic leaders win seasons. The hardest version of this conversation is with your best performer. Top performers resist structure because it feels like a constraint. They will say rhythm slows them down. That resistance is predictable. The rhythm is not there to slow them down. It is there to make their success repeatable without burning them out. The system protects them as much as it protects the team. When leaders create exceptions for top performers, the system collapses for everyone else. No exceptions. The rhythm protects everyone equally.

When rhythm breaks badly enough that more than one part of the system is failing, the response is not to add more. It is to subtract. Stop advanced initiatives. Protect only the core cadence. Reinstall Monday, Tuesday, Wednesday, Thursday and Friday. Do not add complexity until the foundation holds for four consecutive weeks. That is not failure. That is a strategic correction.

You will know rhythm is working before you measure it.

Fewer emotional swings.

Fewer repeated conversations.

Less pressure packed into every decision.

And performance no longer depends on the leader's constant presence.

The system carries more.

The leader carries less.

Rhythm does not eliminate volatility.

Markets shift. People struggle. Results move.

Rhythm prevents those realities from running the system.

When cadence holds, stability becomes embedded instead of enforced.

Rhythm sits where it does because nothing else scales without it. Without rhythm, influence breaks under pressure.

Without rhythm, structure gets skipped when urgency rises.

Without rhythm, momentum turns into motion without direction.

This is why average teams sometimes outperform talented ones.

One relies on effort.

The other relies on rhythm.

If you remember one thing from this Law, remember this.

Stability is not created by intensity.

It is created by return.

When leaders protect rhythm, performance settles. When they don't, instability fills the gap.

That is not a preference.

It is a law.

---

**LESSON IN A BREATH**

*Cadence creates confidence. The week needs a beat before the numbers can rise.*

---

Cadence creates confidence. The week needs a beat before the numbers can rise.

### Endnotes: Rhythm

[1] Temporal Predictability and Team Performance Structured weekly rhythms reduce cognitive load, improve decision speed, and increase collective performance by stabilizing emotional variance. [2] Cadence and Performance Drift Consistent weekly cadences reduce performance drift by reinforcing behavioral expectations and shortening feedback loops. [3] Predictable Sequencing and Executive Function Predictable sequencing reduces anxiety and increases executive function, enabling clearer reasoning during high-stakes interactions.

# Chapter 11: Law 2 – The Box

## Law 2: The Box

*Qualify, Prioritize, Strategize, Close*

| Value | Need |
|---|---|
| Outcomes, ROI, Results | Pain, Urgency, Cost of Inaction |
| **Decision Maker** | **Affordability** |
| Authority, Access, Alignment | Budget, Investment, Fit |

*Law 2: The Box – Qualify, Prioritize, Strategize, Close*

In the Acura conference room, objections sounded different but felt the same. We kept arguing with surface problems while the real hesitation sat underneath, unnamed. The Box gave it an address.

The Box governs decision containment.

Most decisions don't fall apart because people are difficult.

They fall apart because the conversation is loose.

When nothing contains a decision, everything gets dragged into it. Opinions widen. Emotions rise. Discussions loop. Judgment doesn't improve. It just gets louder.

That's the problem the Box solves. At Acura, I wasn't trying to invent a framework. I was trying to stop every conversation from turning into an argument. We kept getting stuck on objections that sounded different but felt the same.

That's when the Box showed up.

The Box wasn't theoretical. It was practical.

Every stalled conversation landed in one of four places.

Value.

Need.

Decision Makers.

Affordability.

Once we knew the square, everything changed.

We stopped arguing with surface objections and started working the real issue. The conversation calmed down because it finally had edges.

Before the Box, decisions felt personal.

People defended positions. Leaders mediated tone. Progress depended on who spoke last or loudest.

It wasn't a talent problem.

It was an uncontained decision.

The Box does something simple.

It contains the conversation before it invites opinion.

Instead of asking, "What do you think?" It asks, "Which square are we in?" That one move removes emotion from judgment without removing people from the room.

At DirectBuy, scale exposed what happens when the Box is missing. The same problems landed in different squares depending on who handled them. Leaders filled the gaps with opinion, and rework followed.

The Box hadn't disappeared.

It just hadn't been shared.

When decision containment is missing, organizations drift into debate culture.

Every issue feels urgent. Every exception feels personal. Every conversation reopens what should already be closed.

People confuse involvement with progress.

The Box stops that. In higher education, the Box had to be explicit. Value, Need, Decision Makers, and Affordability were clearly defined. Escalation rules were clear. Judgment stabilized without micromanagement.

That wasn't control.

That was containment.

## The Four Squares

The Box holds four decisions. Each one explains a different kind of hesitation. Together, they explain why people pause, stall, or withdraw. Once you know the square, you know where to work next.

Value is the decision to believe. It answers the question, "Is this genuinely better than what I'm doing now?" People rarely compare prices first. They compare confidence. When someone says a solution is too expensive, they usually mean something else looks more dependable, more trustworthy, or more certain to deliver the outcome they want. Price becomes the language for emotional comparison.

Value breaks down when the prospect believes the new direction is not meaningfully better than the current one. Until they believe it is better, every discussion about cost is premature.

Need establishes urgency. Someone may love the idea, appreciate the outcome, and understand the benefit, but still not act because the timing feels flexible. Human beings delay decisions that do not feel connected to a necessary change. When people say they "need to think about it," they often mean nothing in their current situation feels pressing enough to justify movement. Need becomes real when people connect today's decision to something they can no longer postpone. Without that connection, motion stalls.

Decision Makers Decisions depend on who holds authority, influence, and emotional weight. A partner, spouse, parent, boss, or colleague may serve as the real decision maker even if they are not present. When the person in the room cannot commit without someone else's involvement, hesitation is not resistance. It is structural.

Momentum collapses when teams and salespeople try to close the wrong person harder. If the true decision maker is not engaged, no amount of persuasion creates movement. You do not have a decision. You have a preview of a decision.

Affordability is not about price. It is about fit. Someone wants the solution, believes in its value, and feels the timing is right. Now they need to integrate the choice into their real life without creating strain. When they object primarily to the price, it often means they already satisfied the other three squares.

The mistake is trying to solve Affordability first. Discounts, concessions, and urgency tactics rarely work if Value, Need, and Decision Makers are not already aligned. You cannot fix timing with price. You cannot fix confidence with a discount. You cannot fix the wrong audience by offering a smaller payment.

## Why The Box Works

The Box works because it gives people language. Most hesitations are emotional before they become verbal. People know something is holding them back but cannot always articulate exactly why. When you name the hesitation clearly, they stop defending and start clarifying.

The Box removes pressure. Instead of pushing for a close, you are diagnosing what is happening in the conversation. Leaders who use the Box consistently reduce confusion, avoid misalignment, and prevent unnecessary escalation. Teams begin to recognize that hesitation is not rejection. It is information.

The Box lowers tension by making the next step obvious. Once you know the square, you know the corrective action. The clarity alone often moves the conversation forward.

## How to Use The Box

Step 1: Ask.

You invite true hesitation into the room.

"So I understand, is the question more about the right fit or more about the right time?" "What part of the decision feels unclear?" "What else needs to be considered before this becomes real?" Open questions signal safety. People reveal the genuine problem when they stop feeling evaluated.

Step 2: Simplify the concern.

You rephrase what you heard in short form and place it in a square.

"It sounds like the hesitation is timing. Does that feel accurate?" "It sounds like the key question is value compared to your other options. Fair?" "It sounds like we need the other decision maker in the room before this can move forward. Right?" This is not pressure. It is clarity. It allows the other person to correct you or confirm what is true.

Step 3: Let Them Answer.

Once they confirm the square, you ask a clarifying question that helps them think clearly. "What would push this from a want to a need?" "What would make this direction feel meaningfully better than your current plan?" "What would waiting change realistically?" "What would make this feel financially responsible instead of stressful?" The shift happens when they hear their own reasoning. You are not convincing. You are allowing clarity to surface.

## Common Box Mistakes

Solving Affordability First.

Leaders reduce prices or increase incentives when the real issue is confidence, timing, or the absence of the true decision maker. These changes feel desperate when they do not match the underlying hesitation.

Skipping Decision Makers.

A strong conversation with the wrong person produces false momentum. Without the decision maker, you do not have a decision. You have a preview of a decision.

Treating Need as Value.

People nod along, agree, smile, and still delay because they do not feel urgency. More information does not fix a Need problem. People move when they see why waiting creates a consequence.

Pushing Past Value.

If someone believes a competitor is more credible, lowering your price does not work. Until confidence shifts, no financial structure creates movement.

## The Box in Practice

A couple finishes a presentation. They like what they heard, but something is holding them back. The husband says, "We need to think about it."

Step 1: Ask.

"Of course. When you think about it, is it more about whether this is the right fit, or more about whether now is the right time?" Step 2: Simplify.

"So it sounds like the real question is timing, not confidence in the program. Fair?" Step 3: Let Them Answer.

"What would waiting another six months change for you?" They answer honestly. They see that the pattern of delay is the real barrier. Movement happens because clarity replaces pressure.

This is the essence of the Box. It does not create persuasion. It creates understanding. Understanding creates motion.

## Using The Box as an Ongoing Diagnostic

The Box is not a closing technique. It is a leadership habit. The same diagnostic that works in a sales conversation works in a team meeting, a one-on-one, a midweek check-in, or a quarterly review. Wherever decisions stall, the Box tells you why.

The simplest team diagnostic is this: when someone reports that a conversation, a deal, or a project is stalled, do not ask for solutions. Ask which square of the Box holds the hesitation. That one question trains your team to stop interpreting friction as failure and start using it as a signal. A stalled conversation becomes a map. Once they can name the hesitation, they can solve it.[1] When the same square keeps appearing across multiple stalled interactions, you are looking at a system problem, not an individual one. If every rep is stuck on Value, the messaging is wrong. If every deal stalls at Decision Makers, the process is reaching the wrong people. If Affordability keeps surfacing before the other three squares are closed, someone is rushing the sequence. The pattern tells you where to work.

The Box Check is one of the fastest ways to find out what is breaking. Take ten stalled interactions. Place each hesitation into a square. Look at the pattern. Within an hour, you will know whether the problem is language, targeting, sequencing, or something else entirely. Most leaders skip this step because they think they already know the answer. They usually do not.

## What The Box Requires

The Box sits atop trust. It cannot function when people feel unsafe or evaluated. If someone does not trust you, they will not reveal their true hesitation. They will offer surface answers to protect themselves. Without trust, clarity collapses, and the best diagnostic tool becomes ineffective.

The Box requires calm leadership, patient questioning, and a willingness to listen without steering. Concerns are not obstacles. They are signals. When you see hesitation as information instead of resistance, you create enough safety for people to be honest about what is happening.

The Box clarifies direction. ICE determines whether anyone will walk in that direction with you.

Without Influence, they won't tell you who really decides.

Without Confidence, they won't believe your solution is better.

Without Empathy, they won't reveal their real hesitation.

The map may be accurate, but without ICE, the car has four flat tires. The Box doesn't eliminate disagreement.

It limits where disagreement belongs.

When the boundaries are clear, people think better inside them. Decisions hold because they were framed intentionally. Leaders stop refereeing and start trusting the system.

This is why the Box matters.

Clarity without containment creates debate.

Containment creates usable clarity.

Without the Box, momentum stalls. Reciprocity turns emotional. Rhythm becomes rigid.

Everything feels heavier than it should.

If you remember one thing from this Law, remember this.

Decisions fall apart when nothing contains them.

Judgment improves when boundaries come first.

The Box governs whether decisions stabilize or drift.

It is a law.

---

**LESSON IN A BREATH**

*Every hesitation has an address. When you know the square, you know the next step.*

---

Every hesitation has an address. When you know the square, you know the next step.

### Endnotes: The Box

[1] Emotional Safety and Disclosure People disclose more accurate information when they perceive the environment as emotionally safe, reducing defensive reasoning and increasing clarity during decision-making.

# Chapter 12: Law 1 – ICE

## Law 1: ICE

*Influence, Confidence, Empathy*

*Law 1: ICE – Influence, Confidence, Empathy*

On the Honda lot, the moment before I spoke mattered more than the words that followed. Pace synced before clarity. Trust formed before information transferred. Skip that order, and nothing holds.

Influence comes before clarity. Clarity comes before commitment.

If you have ever walked away from a conversation thinking you were clear, only to realize later that nothing actually changed, you have already felt this Law at work.

Leaders routinely assume that if they explain something well enough, people will understand it. And if people understand it, they will act on it. That assumption feels reasonable. It is also wrong more often than we want to admit. What breaks the chain is not intelligence.

It is influence.

People do not resist clarity. They resist direction that arrives before trust.

That is what ICE governs.

On the Honda lot, standing side by side at the car, the moment before I spoke mattered more than the words that followed.

Influence is the precondition for accuracy.

Until someone feels safe with you, what they share is filtered. Answers get shorter. Agreement comes too quickly. Questions go vague. People protect themselves without announcing it.

Leaders misread this as alignment.

It is not.

It is compliance without commitment.

At this point, many people assume ICE is just another way of saying Like, Trust, and Understand.

It is not.

Like, Trust, and Understand are experiences. They are what people feel in a conversation. You know when they are present and when they are not.

ICE is the system that governs those experiences.

People can like you without giving you influence. People can trust you without fully understanding you. People can say they understand and still not act.

That is where leaders get fooled. ICE names the sequence that makes those experiences reliable. Like creates safety. Trust creates permission. Only then does understanding become accurate enough to hold.

When the order is right, movement follows. When the order is wrong, everything feels fine until it does not.

Like, Trust, and Understand is the result. It's what someone feels when they sit across from you. Do I like this person? Do I trust them? Do I get what they're saying?

ICE is how you get there. You build real interest first, then bring clarity, and only then move to action. If you rush the order, clarity feels like pressure, and trust drops fast.

Like, Trust, and Understand describe what is happening in the room. ICE tells you whether what is happening will hold under pressure.

Without ICE, Like turns into friendliness without influence. Trust turns into goodwill without honesty. Understanding turns into nodding without commitment. ICE does not add a new concept. It explains why the old ones break.

In the shoelace test, pace synchronized before explanation, and that same order determines whether clarity holds here.

Most breakdowns that get labeled as communication problems are actually sequence problems.

Leaders push for understanding before influence is established. They correct before trust is earned. They solve before permission is granted.

It feels efficient. It feels helpful. It often feels necessary.

What it produces is resistance that has no language.

People nod. They agree. They do not follow through.

The leader leaves confused.

The team leaves guarded.

ICE explains why.

## Why the Order Cannot Be Reversed

The brain filters information through the lens of emotional safety. If safety is absent, logic never gets a turn.[1] You must follow the sequence every time.

First, they decide if you are safe.

Then, they decide if you are credible.

Only then do they consider what you are saying.

Trying to skip ahead creates pressure. Pressure creates resistance. Resistance kills movement.

Influence is not persuasion. Confidence is not dominance. Empathy is not agreement. Each is a signal the other person uses to determine whether they can think clearly in your presence.

## The Three Components of ICE

Influence: Will They Follow When You Stop? Influence is not authority. It is not charisma. It is the moment someone unconsciously stays close enough to listen.

On the Honda lot, I learned that matching someone's pace creates micro-alignment. When an older couple walked slowly, I matched them. When they paused, I paused. Their breathing slowed. Their shoulders dropped. They felt understood without a single sentence being exchanged. The actual test came when I stopped walking to examine a car. If they stopped with me, we had already formed a connection. They had granted me influence. If they kept moving, they were still protecting themselves.

Influence is built through alignment, not control.

You create alignment by matching their tempo long enough for them to match yours.[2] The same principle holds in any leadership conversation. Do they re-engage when you pause, or do they use the pause to disengage? Do they move toward you or away from you when a choice appears? Are they following your lead without being asked, or only when directed? Those are not personality questions. They are influence diagnostics. And they tell you whether anything you say next will actually land.

Influence is the permission to lead. Without it, nothing that follows will hold.

Confidence: Do They Think Clearly in Your Presence? Confidence is not about projecting strength. It is about the other person feeling calm enough to stop performing and tell you the truth. This is their confidence in the interaction, not yours in the outcome.

On the Honda floor, couples often put on a performance. They acted decisively, informed, and certain. But the performance blocked clarity. When I slowed down, or when I stepped back to give them space, something shifted. They started asking real questions. They stopped posturing. They became themselves.

Confidence is the emotional state that lets someone think clearly.

If your presence raises anxiety, they cannot process information. If your presence reduces anxiety, they open up. Your emotional tone becomes theirs. Leaders forget this. Teams absorb the leader's internal weather long before they absorb the leader's instructions.[3] You can see it in every structured moment. The one-on-one. The team reflection. The midweek check-in. Every coaching conversation either builds confidence or chips away at it. When someone surfaces a challenge, the instinct is to jump into solution mode. "Here's what you should do." That feels efficient. What it actually builds is dependency. Fixing reinforces dependency and erodes the very confidence you need your people to develop.

The better move: "If you were coaching me through this, what would you tell me to do first?" Their answer reveals the real obstacle. It also strengthens their ability to self-correct. Confidence grows when people solve problems in your presence, not when you solve problems for them.

Watch for whether they volunteer new information without being asked. Whether they openly admit uncertainty. Whether they process decisions more clearly as the conversation continues or shut down. Those signals tell you whether confidence is building or decaying. They show up long before results do.

Confidence is the space where truth replaces performance.

Empathy: Do You See Their Square Before They Name It? Empathy is not sweetness. It is not agreement. It is accuracy.

Remember the Friday night couple who had been to every dealership. Their surface concern was features and warranty. The real hesitation, the one they had been carrying into every lot, was financial fear from a rough year. Because I asked one honest question instead of pushing through their excuses, the truth surfaced. That is empathy. Not sweetness. Accuracy.

Empathy is the ability to detect the real square they are standing on before they say it. The Box depends on this. Rhythm depends on this. Momentum depends on this. Reciprocity depends on this. Every system fails when empathy is inaccurate.

Signals of hidden hesitation show up early. A subject change. A shift in tone. A question that does not match the moment. When you miss those signals, you end up diagnosing the wrong problem. When you diagnose the wrong problem, the Box collapses.

The diagnostic is not complicated, but it requires patience. When someone says "I'm fine" and their body says otherwise, pause. Give it three seconds. Then ask, "What's the thing you're not saying?" Most leaders skip this step because silence feels unproductive. It is not. Silence is where real answers surface. People start sharing concerns before they become crises when they believe you are actually listening. You catch problems in the hesitation phase, not the breakdown phase.

Do you know what they are worried about, or only what they said out loud? Can you name their constraint before they do? Do their shoulders relax as they talk, or tighten? Do they feel understood or merely heard?

Empathy is not softness. It is precision.

## Common ICE Breakdowns

Most breakdowns are not total failures. They are imbalances. Each imbalance points directly to the repair.

High Confidence, Low Influence: The Bulldozer.

You know the way, but no one comes with you. People nod in meetings, then change nothing. You push harder and assume resistance is laziness when it is misalignment.

Repair: Build Influence first. Slow your pace. Ask better questions. Match their tempo before you try to set it.

High Empathy, Low Confidence: The Approval-Seeker. You are well-liked but ineffective. You avoid discomfort. You soften clarity to protect feelings.

Repair: Build Confidence. Decide what they need from you more than what you want them to feel about you.

High Influence, Low Empathy: The Disconnected Leader.

People follow you, but the outcomes do not improve. You rely on past patterns instead of the present truth.

Repair: Rebuild Empathy. Get closer to the authentic experience. Ask questions from the ground, not the assumption.

Each imbalance reveals the next step in your leadership development. ICE is not a personality trait. It is a discipline.

## ICE in Practice

ICE is not something you build once and walk away from. It requires ongoing attention. Every interaction either reinforces the sequence or weakens it.

The simplest diagnostic is the ICE Check. Sit with each person on your team. Ask only, "How are you doing?" Then listen without offering solutions. Watch for what surfaces and what stays hidden. If people give you real answers, ICE is holding. If they perform for you, it is not.

When team meetings become a place for reporting numbers instead of sharing learning, ICE is eroding. The team performs instead of thinking. They tell you what you want to hear instead of what they actually learned. The fix is not more structure. The fix is more silence. Let them articulate what happened instead of waiting for you to interpret it. For remote and hybrid teams, ICE requires visibility. You cannot diagnose tone, stress, or hesitation through audio alone. Video is not optional for the conversations that matter. Silence on a screen is not neutral. It is diagnostic. If engagement drops, ICE is compromised.

When the system feels like it is breaking and you cannot identify where to start, start here. Meet with each person for fifteen minutes. Ask how they are doing. Listen without solutions. Within a day you will know whether trust is intact or whether it has been quietly eroding underneath the results. If trust is intact, the other laws can be repaired. If trust has gone, nothing else holds until you restore it.

## Why ICE Is the Foundation

Every breakdown in every Law traces back to ICE.

Collapse happens when ICE erodes. When trust fades, systems stop holding. Reciprocity fails without ICE. Service without trust looks like manipulation. Momentum stalls without ICE. Visibility cannot compensate for a culture that does not believe its leader. Rhythm breaks without ICE. People abandon cadence when they no longer trust its purpose. The Box dies without ICE. If they do not feel safe, they will not tell you the truth, and you will solve the wrong problem.■ ICE determines whether everything above it becomes a system or a struggle.

ICE does not slow progress. It prevents rework.

When you earn Like, people relax.

When you build Trust, people tell the truth.

When you reach Understanding, decisions hold.

That order is not optional.

It is structural.

ICE is the foundation everything else rests on.

Without influence, the Box produces guesses.

Without trust, Rhythm collapses under pressure.

Without understanding, Momentum decays into activity.

This is why ICE sits first.

Not because it is impressive.

Because nothing else survives without it.

If you remember one thing from this Law, remember this.

Clarity delivered too early feels like pressure.

Clarity delivered in sequence feels like leadership.

That is ICE.

---

**LESSON IN A BREATH**

*You cannot transfer clarity until you first create safety.*

---

You cannot transfer clarity until you first create safety.

**Endnotes: ICE**

[1] Trust and Cognitive Reception Information from untrusted sources triggers defensive cognitive patterns, reducing comprehension and increasing resistance. [2] Mirroring and Threat Reduction Behavioral mirroring increases relational alignment and reduces perceived threat responses in first-time interactions. [3] Emotional Contagion in Leadership Leaders transfer mood and tension long before they transfer instructions. - Psychological Safety as Gatekeeper Edmondson, A. C. "Psychological Safety and Learning Behavior in Work Teams," Administrative Science Quarterly. Emotional safety remains the primary gatekeeper for learning and decision-making across social and organizational contexts.

# Chapter 13: How the Laws Work Together

I didn't discover these Laws in order. I ran into them one at a time, usually after something broke.

What took longer to see is that they weren't separate ideas. They were one system, showing itself under different kinds of pressure. Each Law solved a problem that only became visible after the one before it had been addressed.

That's why the order matters.

You don't start at Law 1.

You start where everyone actually starts.

You start at Collapse.

Collapse is the moment you realize success is fragile. Things are working, but only because you're involved. The system hasn't failed. It just hasn't finished.

Once you see that, the next question shows up on its own.

Why am I still carrying so much of this?

That's where Reciprocity enters. It determines whether ownership actually moves back across the line or quietly stays with the leader. When ownership begins to return, effort usually increases. People care more. Responsibility spreads. Most leaders expect that to feel like relief.

It rarely does.

That's because effort still isn't stacking.

That's the problem Momentum solves. Momentum determines whether yesterday actually matters today. Without it, teams work hard and still feel like they're starting over.

When effort finally compounds, progress begins to settle. Not because anyone pushes harder, but because something begins to give back.

That return is Rhythm.

Rhythm replaces spikes with consistency. It turns momentum into something people can rely on. Progress stops feeling dramatic and starts feeling dependable. Once things stabilize, a new friction appears.

Decisions begin to feel heavier than they should.

That's where The Box comes in. The Box contains decisions so judgment doesn't spill into debate, emotion, and rework. It protects stability from slowly eroding.

Only after all of that does ICE fully make sense.

ICE governs how conversations move. It explains why clarity sometimes creates pressure instead of trust. When the rest of the system is in place, ICE feels natural. Conversations move because the system can support them.

This isn't a model to memorize.

It's a way to see what's actually happening.

Once you see it, you stop trying to fix people and start finishing systems.

# Chapter 14: The Wave Starts Monday

You've read the stories. You've seen the Laws. Now comes the only part that matters: what you do next.

Not next month. Not when things calm down. Monday.

The leaders who transform their teams don't wait for perfect conditions. They don't wait for buy-in. They don't wait for permission.

They start.

One Monday Reflection. One Tuesday, 1:1, where you listen. One moment, when you diagnose the real objection rather than guessing. One week where you protect the rhythm instead of breaking it for a "quick win." That's how it begins. Not with a revolution. With a rhythm.

## The Choice

Every leader eventually faces the same decision:

Will you be the hero who holds everything together?

Or will you build something that holds itself?

The Six Laws gave it a name. Now you give it a home.

Show up Monday morning with one question for your team: "What did we learn last week that we need to protect this week?" Then listen.

That's the Monday Reflection. That's where it starts. That's the first ripple in the wave.

# Chapter 15: The Rhythm Wave in Action

Theory is comfortable. Deployment is where it gets real. Here is what it looked like when the system was installed in four different environments.

## The Franchise That Stopped Needing Rescue

When I owned three franchise locations in New York and Boston, the first operation ran well because I was there every day. The second wobbled every time I left. The third nearly broke me.

The problem was not talent. The problem was that every decision waited for me. I was the bottleneck disguised as the leader. Classic hero dependency.

The fix started with the Box. I trained my managers to diagnose stalled conversations themselves instead of escalating every hesitation to me. Within weeks, they stopped calling for answers and started calling with solutions. Then I installed the Five-Day Flow. Monday reflections. Tuesday coaching. Wednesday calibration. Once the cadence held, I could step back without the system stepping backward. Those three locations became three of the top ten performing franchises in a 160-location national system. Not because I worked harder. Because the rhythm replaced me.

Laws deployed: The Box (Law 2), Rhythm (Law 3), Collapse prevention (Law 6).

## The Sales Division Built from Nothing

At International Cruise and Excursions, we launched a face-to-face sales model that did not exist before we built it. No playbook. No predecessor. No template. Just an idea and a kiosk in a shopping center.

ICE (the law, not the company) came first. We could not sell travel memberships to people walking past a kiosk by shouting at them. We had to build influence before we asked for anything. That meant giving first. Helping someone with their bags. Offering a genuine conversation instead of a pitch. Reciprocity followed naturally. When people felt served instead of sold, they opened the door themselves.

As we scaled from one location to six offices across Arizona, New York, New Jersey, Pennsylvania, and California, the system had to travel without me. Momentum tracking gave visibility across distance. The weekly rhythm kept remote teams aligned. The result was twenty percent year-over-year growth, consistently, and a division that reached over twenty million dollars in annual revenue.

Laws deployed: ICE (Law 1), Reciprocity (Law 5), Momentum (Law 4), Rhythm (Law 3).

## The Campus That Held Through a Pay Cut

In higher education, I managed over one hundred admissions representatives across fifteen campuses. We were delivering ten percent annual growth in enrollment and revenue for three straight years. Then the company reduced compensation by fifteen percent.

That is a collapse trigger. When people feel betrayed by the organization, trust erodes. When trust erodes, rhythm breaks. When rhythm breaks, performance follows.

We did not try to spin it. We told the truth. We acknowledged the frustration. Then we rebuilt ICE from the ground up. Not through speeches. Through presence. Campus visits. Honest one-on-ones. Listening before fixing. We protected the Monday reflections and the Tuesday coaching sessions even when everything felt unstable. The rhythm did not make the pay cut feel fair. But it gave people something stable to return to when everything else felt uncertain.

Team engagement held. Productivity held. Channel revenue still increased fifteen percent that fiscal year. The system survived because it was built on trust, not incentives.

Laws deployed: ICE (Law 1), Rhythm (Law 3), Collapse prevention (Law 6).

## The Remote Team That Learned to See

When I was coaching sales managers across five states, every problem started the same way. A manager would call and say something was off. Close rates were down. Energy was flat. They did not know why.

The old approach was to diagnose it for them. Tell them what to fix. That worked for a week. Then a new problem showed up and they called again. I was the system. The moment I stopped answering, the system stopped working. The shift came when I stopped giving answers and started asking questions. "What do you think changed?" "Have you watched them?" "Where in the Box does the hesitation live?" Within months, managers stopped calling for permission to act. They called to tell me what they had already fixed. Reciprocity had moved. Ownership had transferred. They were coaching their teams the same way I had coached them.

That is what it looks like when the system finishes itself.

Laws deployed: Reciprocity (Law 5), The Box (Law 2), ICE (Law 1).

Four environments. Different industries, different team sizes, different pressures. Same principles. Same results. The wave does not care about the context. It cares about the conditions.

## A Final Word

If you made it this far, thank you.

Not for finishing a book, but for staying with the work long enough to recognize yourself in it. That tells me something about how you lead, or how you want to. I didn't write this because I had answers early. I wrote it because I spent a long time not having them. I learned this system in motion, under pressure, while trying to do good work without becoming someone I didn't respect. I learned it by failing publicly and figuring things out in real time.

What you've just read is not a theory I polished after the fact. It's the record of what held when everything else didn't.

Across different industries, different teams, different seasons of my life, the same truth kept showing up. When people rely on heroes, things break. When people rely on rhythm, things hold.

That applies to sales teams and classrooms. To boardrooms and kitchens. To parents, coaches, founders, and leaders who carry more than they let on.

You don't need to be louder to lead better.

You don't need to work harder to create consistency.

You don't need more pressure, more urgency, or more intensity.

You need rhythm.

If this book did its job, it didn't inspire you. It calmed you. It gave you language for things you already felt. It showed you that stability is built, not hoped for, and that systems earn trust better than speeches ever will.

You don't have to install everything at once. In fact, you shouldn't. Protect one rhythm. Ask one better question. Slow one moment down enough to see what's actually happening.

And know this: drift will come. Not because the system failed, but because it worked well enough that you'll stop thinking about it. That's the trap. Every leader I've ever coached hit that moment. The ones who lasted weren't the ones who never drifted. They were the ones who caught it early and came back to the rhythm before the rhythm forgot them.

That's how this starts. Not with a big announcement.

Not with a reset.

Not with a perfect plan.

It starts Monday.

Show up with curiosity instead of control.

Listen before you fix. Build the system so you don't have to be the system.

And when the work begins to hold without you, when people move with confidence instead of waiting for rescue, when the chaos quiets and the rhythm takes over, you'll know.

That's the wave.

Thank you for trusting me with your time. Now go build something that lasts.

Kevin Cover For leaders ready to install the Six Laws, a free 90-Day Implementation Guide is available at rhythmleadershipgroup.com.

www.ingramcontent.com/pod-product-compliance
Lightning Source LLC
Chambersburg PA
CBHW051312220526
45468CB00004B/1314